Soul Pearls

Worship Resources
for the Black Church

Cheryl A. Kirk-Duggan

Abingdon Press
Nashville

SOUL PEARLS
WORSHIP RESOURCES FOR THE BLACK CHURCH

Copyright © 2003 by Cheryl A. Kirk-Duggan

This book is printed on recycled, acid-free, elemental-chlorine–free paper.

Library of Congress Cataloging-in-Publication Data

Kirk-Duggan, Cheryl A.
  Soul Pearls: worship resources for the black church /
Cheryl A. Kirk-Duggan.
    p. cm.
Includes index.
  ISBN 0-687-05157-6 (pbk.: alk. paper)
1. African American public worship.   2. Worship programs.   I. Title.

BR563.N4 K58 2003
264′.0089′96073—dc21   2003000657

All scripture quotations unless noted otherwise are taken from the *Revised Standard
Version of the Bible*, copyright 1946, 1952, 1971 by the Division of Christian Education of
the National Council of the Churches of Christ in the United States of America. Used
by permission. All rights reserved.

Scripture quotations noted (NASB) are taken from the NEW AMERICAN STAN-
DARD BIBLE®, © Copyright The Lockman Foundation 1960, 1962, 1963, 1968, 1971,
1972, 1973, 1975, 1977. Used by permission.

Scripture quotations noted (NIV) are taken from the HOLY BIBLE: NEW INTERNA-
TIONAL VERSION®. Copyright © 1973, 1978, 1984 by the International Bible Society.
Used by permission of Zondervan Publishing House. All rights reserved.

03 04 05 06 07 08 09 10 11 12 — 10 9 8 7 6 5 4 3 2 1

MANUFACTURED IN THE UNITED STATES OF AMERICA

Contents

PART III: EMOTIONAL LANDSCAPES

PART IV: EMPOWERMENT

PART V: HUMAN VIRTUES

PART VI: INSTITUTIONS

PART VII: SOCIOPOLITICAL FOCUS

PART VIII: SPIRITUAL WONDERS

Acknowledgments

To Melinda, my maternal great grandmother who was found,
after being abandoned, on the banks of the Mississippi River

To the Bishops, Presiding Elders, Ministers, Leaders, and all
Laypersons of the Christian Methodist Episcopal Church

To all Sunday School Teachers
who plant deep the foundations of who we are

To all Choir Directors who teach us to cherish
the words and make a joyful noise unto God

Special thanks to Abingdon Press for blessing me with the gift
of developing this project. Thanks to those pastors, congregations, friends, and family members who have been models of God
before me, allowing my spiritual imagination to soar and glean
from my life experiences as I reflected on and then developed the
material in this volume. Blessings and thanks to those leaders
who will embrace this book and make it their own. Thanks be to
God, for an opportunity to once more effect hope, to inspire, and
share the prophetic, the liturgical, the artistic, and the health-
wise with God's people. And, as always, my eternal thanks and
love to my best friend, stringer, designated driver, house spouse,
and beloved husband: "Reverse" Mike, who shares me with the
world, who understands my call/demand from a loving God to
write, who casts a keen editorial eye over the completed manu-
script, and who remains totally, completely, and utterly responsible for all errors, misattributions, typos, and omissions herein,
who keeps me laughing, who reminds me to hear well, who
insists that I not fret over small things, and reminds me that all
things are small.

Introduction

Soul is the toughness born of hard times, soul is what the compassion-oppressed people develop after centuries of sharing a loaf that is never enough. Soul is a special sister/brotherhood of those set apart from their fellows, made visible by physical appearance and different customs. Soul is graceful survival under impossible circumstances.[1]

For many, the term *soul* connotes things of the spirit. Some hear the smoky, rhythm and blues tunes of the 1960s and 1970s. In 2003, those melodies are still played on radio programs that feature oldies and goldies. That same genre continues to be conjured up in the likes of Aretha Franklin, Teddy Pendergrass, Luther Vandross, Gladys Knight, Stevie Wonder, and a host of other vocalists and instrumentalists who play R&B and/or jazz, like Wynton Marsalis, BB King, and Quincy Jones. For some folk, the term *soul* elicits smells from the kitchen in Big Mama's house: collard greens, dressing, hot water cornbread, biscuits, peach cobbler, turkey—depending upon your geographic location and the place from which your family migrated. For persons

---

1. William H. Grier, M.D. and Price M. Cobbs, M.D., *The Jesus Bag* (New York: McGraw Hill, 1971), 55.

who connect with the psychological and the spiritual, soul pertains to that place which makes us uniquely human, the intersection of mind and morality where feelings emerge; the originating place of decisions, of right and wrong; the locus of deep self-awareness. Thus one can sing "My Soul's Been Anchored in the Lord," and "It Is Well with My Soul," to name a place of certainty, comfort, and peace. One can speak of the "dark night of the soul," or the "damnation of the soul" to convey deep distress, hopelessness, major depression, and a harsh sense of condemnation. Many souls are wounded and injured; others know unspeakable joy and great delight in God and life.

Soul Pearls, as a liturgical manual, acknowledges the power of the soul through fifty-two themes that are part of celebrating who we are and whose we are. One's soul is the immaterial essence, the animating principle that makes us who we are. Our soul is the spiritual standard or principle embodied in human beings, all rational and spiritual beings, or the universe. Pearls are a dense, variously colored, and usually lustrous substance formed of concentric layers of nacre. They begin as an abnormal growth within the shell of some mollusks (e.g., oysters), and are used as gems. Thus pearls are stones that many use in jewelry. God's entire creation is a cornucopia of beauty, including stones or gems deemed very choice or precious. *Soul Pearls* is a thematic liturgical volume created to assist pastors, worship leaders, and worship committees in bringing new fervor and focus to their worship events. The fifty-two themes are issues that African Americans face in daily life, but often are not the focus of the sermon. To invigorate services, or to help prepare for the upcoming services, one can use this volume as commentary, as guide, as resource for a vital and effective worship experience. Each theme includes *a selected scripture, a quotation from an African or African American, an invocation or opening prayer, reflections, a prayer for the community, a litany,* and *a benediction. Soul Pearls* is designed with flexibility in mind. The topics can be tailored for use in a variety of settings such as worship services, Bible studies, Sunday school classes, or retreats.

Part I—Balanced Living

---

1. The Body/Sensuality

Shun immorality. Every other sin which a [person] commits is outside the body; but the immoral [person] sins against [her/his] own body.
—1 Corinthians 6:18

Quotation

African Americans' existential ambivalence about their bodies may be the most personally painful legacy of slavery and racial oppression in the United States. The consequences of that ambivalence for women may be the most dangerous and debilitating. Black men also have injured self-images but they are able to defend themselves from certain kinds of assaults and have almost nothing to fear in terms of assaults and sexual harassment from women. There are also lucrative outlets for Black men to use their bodies while maintaining tremendous illusions of power and in some cases real power. Most women are as defenseless now as they were during slavery and in some ways they may be more so." (Cheryl Townsend Gilkes, professor, minister, author, religion sociologist)

Invocation

We gather as a collected group of bodies to worship and offer praise; let us experience these bodies as sacred bodies as we come before God with thanksgiving and anticipation. Let us worship God!

Reflections

As we call God holy, and honor God's majestic character, we can honor our own created sacredness, understanding the beauty of our bodies and our bodies' sensuality. So often we live out our faith in synchronization with our thoughts about prayer and a faithful life, without considering the holiness of God that so shapes our lives as children of God. As we embrace this holistic sacredness of ourselves, we can earnestly know the gift of total health. By grace, we can reshape our sense of self and our attitudes, which affect how we live, move, think, and express in the world. Living from the space of embodied sensuality and spirituality imbues us with a love that radiates hope to others. After confessing wrongs perpetrated against us, we have room for needed healing and restoration. Many of us work on our prayer life and our physical health, but we fail to connect the two. This schizophrenic sense of relating to oneself leads to deep pain and a need to grieve because of what has been encoded in our spiritual DNA. There is not a group of people on earth who has not at one time or another faced the annihilation of its family, race, tribe, clan, or nation. We must own up to this pain as we seek total healing and health, and understand that our bodies, with our five senses, are exquisite, sacred, and beautiful.

Prayer

Gracious God of health and life, we bless you for your marvelous works within the human body. You have been so faithful in your creation, that much of what we do comes by training and reflex. We give thanks for the magnificent construction of our bodies, for the wonderful creativity of our minds, and for the ability to live a faithful life of spirituality, using our bodies, minds, and souls. For this we know gratitude unspeakable. Bless us to respect ourselves so that we see taking care of ourselves as a central component of faith. Let us not take any of our gifts and graces for granted; nor let us bring harm or disrespect to the bodies, minds, and souls of others. Anoint us to daily appreciate the gifts of sight, smell, touch, taste, and sound. Help us see the sacramental connection between our faith and health as fundamental components of our spirituality. Bless our caregivers, health practitioners, pastors, ministers, and spiritual directors that they might be loving and proficient in designing our care. Help us hear their diagnoses with faithful, discerning ears. Bless us all and make us one body of the faithful, clearly understanding our lives in light of your call.

Litany

Leader: In all that is within us we bless God. We thank God for the gift of our bodies, and our five senses, created to be whole and complete, to listen to the God embodied within that we may be willing to experience health as a part of our salvation.

People: **For the gift of blessed sensuality, we give thanks. We are grateful for the experience of healthy spirit and body as one expression of God's benevolent care.**

Leader: We give thanks for God's promises that bless us each day as we touch, taste, smell, hear, and see, moving toward an inner peace that comes of a deep spiritual connection with God.

People: **For the gifts of our own physical reality, we rejoice, as our bodies are essential to our hopeful existence. As we honor our sensuality as a part of God's good creation, we embody the sacredness of our bodies, spirits, and minds.**

Leader: The spirituality of God empowers us to be intimate with God, and shapes our own sense of blessed sensuality, moment to moment, and eternally as confessing believers who walk by faith and not by might.

People: **In thanksgiving and fulfillment, we give thanks for the wonderful bodies and marvelous sensuality we experience as a gift; for new ways of being and**

living, we rejoice, as we grow in health, spirit, and
faith, ever praising you, saying holy!

Benediction

As we go now in peace, let us go respecting the bodies, the sacred
temples, of all persons. Let us give witness to this sacredness by all
we say and do. God be with you always; go now in peace. Amen.

2. Community

But if we walk in the light, as [God] is in the light, we have fellowship
[community] with one another.
—1 John 1:7a

Quotation

It is no accident that this homeplace, as fragile and as transi-
tional as it may be, a makeshift shed, a small bit of earth where
one rests, is always subject to violation and destruction. For
when a people no longer have the space to construct homeplace,
we cannot build a meaningful community of resistance." (bell
hooks, feminist, theorist, poet, cultural critic, writer, educator)

Invocation

As we gather in your light—a light of hope, vision, and safe
places—fix our hearts that we may become a community that
resists violence, hatred, and fear; that chooses to stand for love,
justice, and kindness as we come together to praise!

Reflections

In the religious and sociopolitical order and public eye of the United States of America, there is a great deal of discussion around community building with faith-based initiatives, HMOs (Health Maintenance Organizations), comprehensive health care, and health management. Much legislation and public relations focuses on meeting the needs of citizens. Jesus not only engaged in a communal ministry of health and healing, but one of teaching, preaching, and love. As the sacred and secular intermingle, we must nurture an SMO (Spirituality Maintenance Organization) within ourselves and our communities. For some, life is wonderful and they maintain their SMO. For others, thoughts about needing change, about living, and about the inevitability of death open a Pandora's box. Ministry is an invitation to place God front and center. Community is an on-going, dynamic experience of humanity relating with God, and there are hundreds of ways to talk about and embody God. Some define community narrowly as their local congregation, the ministry of the particular congregation. A community is a complex, connected body of individuals who share the interests of living in a particular area. A church community is called to engage, both individually and collectively, in praying daily, visiting the sick, supporting the educational program, and tithing with one's time, money, and other helpful kinds of resources. Healthy ministerial communities involve active engagement with a spiritual landscape designer, God. In God's hands, the planting, fertilizing, irrigating, and pruning of our beings in community moves us to a remarkable place of beauty, humility, and faithfulness.

Prayer

Magnificent God, we are gathered out of the unconsciousness of our collective humanity. You call us to be a community, blessed and anointed to receive salvation, not destruction, at the hands of self or those deemed other. As a growing and vital community, help us learn to share our interests and to make rules and laws in

13

a way that benefit all of society. Let us not know fear as we relate to persons from other faith communities and other races, creeds, or nationalities. Let us not alienate persons because their belief systems are different. Be with us and keep us so that when ignorance, woundedness, fear, and vengeance are our watchwords, we will remember that we are called to live and work together. For you alone are God, you alone are our God. Bless us with spiritual enlightenment, that we may come to know our neighbors and ourselves as true community. Help us see and know and learn differently, that we might not worship at the altars of fear and envy, arrogance and regret. As we grow, help us strive toward a sense of unity with our neighbors.

Litany

Leader: When someone tells us, "Pull yourself up by your own bootstraps," implying that we can go through life and accomplish innumerable tasks by our own willpower, that is, without divine guidance and assistance, we recognize yet again the importance of the wisdom and counsel of our community.

People: **Needing the support of others is not a call for codependent, dysfunctional behavior; community is an opportunity for us all to provide the village that our children, youth, and adults all need for balance and clarity.**

Leader: Needing the support of others is not advocacy for being irresponsible, manipulative, lazy, or abusive. Building community is an opportunity for each of us to extend God's grace within us to a family member or friend.

People: **We have a collective memory and live in communities. With grace, we have the wisdom and the willingness to live healthy, holistic lives in love, sup-**

porting healthy relationships at home and at
work.

Leader: God's grace empowers us to deal with family squabbles
and hostile coworkers. We learn which battles to
fight, which matters are the concern of God, and how
to respond appropriately.

People: **For the sake of community and opportunities to
grow together, we face our fears, our prejudices, and
our flawed perceptions in Christ, that wrongs may
be righted, hearts may be changed, and we might
live together in peace.**

Benediction

As we go forth, one community among hundreds of worshiping
communities, gird our hearts, spirits, and minds to travel the
roads of life in love, sharing your love and the importance of
community at every place we visit, as we radiate your light. God
be with you always; go now in peace. Amen.

—⟋⟍—

3. Evangelism

*The Spirit of the Lord GOD is upon me, /because the LORD has anointed
me /to bring good tidings to the afflicted; /[the Spirit] has sent me to bind up
the brokenhearted, /to proclaim liberty to the captives, /and the opening of
the prison to those who are bound.*
—Isaiah 61:1

Quotation

T he people of God must not be locked in its stained glass fortress with its multicolored windows, red cushioned seats, crimson carpets, temperature-controlled auditorium and Skinner pipe organ where, as Kierkegaard described, 'an anemic preacher preaches an anemic gospel about an anemic Christ to an anemic congregation. . . . The Church gathers to scatter. . . . The Gospel requires us to confess [Jesus] as Savior and that confession implies us to identify with those who are bruised and broken by injustice and oppression and to join with them in efforts of freedom and liberation. If we would be evangelists we must also be agitators where economic condition exploit and political realities deprive people of their God-given right to be free and whole people.' " (William [Bobby] McClain, preacher, author, professor, Civil Rights activist)

Invocation

Beloveds, in this moment we come as a gathered community to meet and praise God, and to recommit our lives to spreading the gospel. Let us rejoice and worship God.

Reflections

A favorite pastime for young children is to sit and listen to someone telling stories, for example, at a library's weekly children's hour. In homes of balance and love, parents, older siblings, and guardians often put children to sleep by reading them a bedtime story. Our lives are stories. Evangelism is an opportunity to share the story of the love of God and the gift of salvation as embodied in Jesus Christ. Sometimes we have an opportunity to share the sense of freedom and wholeness that has come from our life in Christ. In Jesus' earthly ministry, he also told stories; he taught using parables. Evangelism is the process of sharing the good news of the gospel. We share this good news through preaching, teaching, and workshops, in our songs and prayers. We can do some evangelistic work for our congregations by taking the message out to the streets. For some congregations, street ministry and evangelism often occur during revivals. Some congregations are more timid and would rather the "trained" clergy do this work. If we are not doing the Jesus stuff by sharing the good news of the gospel, are we Christians in name only? If we only "walk the walk," that is, live our own lives by the gospel, but do not "talk the talk," that is, share the message, who will tell the story?

Prayer

God, the One who reveals and calls us to teach the gospel, give us the wisdom, courage, and strength to embody evangelism. When we feel that we don't know how to share the gospel, help us see that there is grace in saying "I don't know," and that we need not be embarrassed about not knowing. Help us see that sometimes it is in the not knowing that we actually come to learn and know. Give us the strength to embrace this part of what it means to be a Christian. Some of us are timid because our own faith stories are painful, difficult journeys. Yet, in the middle of these difficulties, many of us have experienced tremendous revelations. These revelations have given us peace and new ways of seeing and of being. Bless us to know and sense those moments that are opportunities. Help us know how to approach people about the gospel in empathy, that we may know what it means to walk in their shoes. Help us to be gracious with every person, never condescending, mean, frightened, or arrogant. Anoint us with a spirit of pastoral teaching. As we learn to share our story with another searching soul, we will all better come to know you and fully experience your grace.

Litany

Leader: What a privilege to go out into our community and share the good news of the gospel. Let us prepare our hearts, minds, souls, and spirits to be the light of Christ to all.

People: We give thanks for the opportunity to spread the gospel. May we do so with joy, honesty, and hope, as a gift of service.

Leader: Blessed are those called to bring the gospel, to evangelize. May each one go out to reach and teach one, and may each be taught and received well, in grace-filled anticipation.

People: We are humbled by the call on our lives to share our experience of faith and reconciliation in Christ Jesus. May our works toward this end speak volumes.

Leader: Throughout the world, our nation, and our community people cry out from spiritual malnutrition. Who will go and live the life of evangelism?

People: By grace, we recommit our lives and ministries to reaching out to bring the gospel message, knowing that we too can experience healing in the process.

Benediction

As believers and messengers of the gospel, we go forth to proclaim the love of God in Christ Jesus, letting our lights shine, radiating back to our Source, Redeemer, and Advocate. God be with you always; go now in peace. Amen.

4. Food/Eating

*And the scribes of the Pharisees, when they saw that he was
eating with sinners and tax collectors, said to his disciples,
"Why does he eat with tax collectors and sinners?"*
—Mark 2:16

Quotation

I don't think it ever occurred to our immediate family to indoc-
trinate children against sharing. Because they had had the
privilege of growing up where they'd raised a lot of food. They
were never hungry. They could share their food with people.
And so, you share your lives with people." (Ella Jo Baker, Civil
Rights activist)

Invocation

Glorious is this day! We come to worship and give thanks for so
many blessings: for life, for family, for health, for joy, for food. As
we envision all life and the gift of food as holy, let us worship God!

Reflections

Sometimes our appetites get us into trouble; other times they
save our lives. Not a day goes by that there is not a report of new
research concerning food, the suggestion of a new diet or food
plan, or a new exercise regime. From such sources as the Centers
for Disease Control and Prevention, the *New England Journal of
Medicine*, and weekly magazines from *Ladies' Home Journal*, to
Time and *Newsweek*, we receive input on vitamins, cholesterol,
antioxidants, preventative and alternative medicines, and
numerous issues about our physical care. When our physical and
emotional appetites outweigh our physical and emotional needs,

we get into trouble. Obesity, addictions, and obsessive/compulsive disorders have escalated. Today, this day, is a call to eat in a healthy, balanced manner based on our age, weight, body mass, and level of exercise. Coupled with a balanced life of faith and health, we can have a wonderful spiritual life with God. Though we can rarely get too much of God, our spiritual focus can become a system of controlling, exclusive, separatist behavior. God calls us to a life of interconnections, balance, and wholeness that helps to shape healthy communities.

Prayer

Blessed Giver of harvests and the fruit of the land, we give thanks for the gifts of food and the opportunities to build relationships over meals. We confess our gratitude for your great bounty. We give thanks for those who plow and plant the fields; harvest and transport the crops; package and sell the food. We give thanks for the resources that enable us to purchase the food that we need. We pray for those who are homeless and are without sustenance. Help us learn how to support those in need without crippling them or wounding their pride and spirit. Give us the wisdom to know what kind of ministries we are called to engage in. May we be intentional about helping feed people's bodies, minds, and spirits; and may we pray for those who die of malnutrition and starvation. Many functions in our spiritual, family, and business life involve food. May we eat only when we are hungry and only those foods that nurture us. May gluttony and compulsive over- and under-eating be named and healed. May we be good stewards of our resources and come to the table for general meals, and to the altar for the Eucharist (Lord's Supper, or Communion) in a spirit of humility, gratitude, hope, and commitment to appreciate the temple of our bodies and the gift of food.

Litany

Leader: What a joy and blessing to have food to eat and to taste so many flavors, the things that are salty, sweet, tart, and sour. How delightful to appreciate the sense of taste.

People: **Blessed is the bounty of God, the food of the earth and the sea, which provides the nutrients and supplements, the vitamins and minerals for our nourishment.**

Leader: How marvelous it is to smell food as it is being prepared, when we have gathered as community, family, and friends. To eat is a delight unto God, a good thing.

People: **Blessed are those who did not have a meal today. May we all become responsible for sharing a meal with the one who is hungry, for our hands are God's hands.**

Leader: We rejoice for the blessing of eating together. We give thanks that we can eat together, appreciate the moment, savor the food, share memories, create new customs of celebration.

People: **As we grow in faith, may we grow in stewardship. As we grow in faith, may we learn to share and to not squander and waste. As we share and serve each other food, may we come to see each meal as a celebration of covenantal love with ourselves, our neighbors, and God.**

Benediction

As we prepare to go out into the world, we give thanks for the gift of food and the joy we experience through eating. May we recommit to feeding those who hunger and thirst after righteousness and those who hunger for food. God be with you always; go now in peace. Amen.

5. Freedom

For you were called to freedom, [brothers and sisters]; only do
not use your freedom as an opportunity for the flesh,
but through love be servants of one another.
—Galatians 5:13

Quotation

For by virtue of a sublime and tortured history lived out on the state of our nation and the world, the Black struggle for freedom, at its best, provides just such openings into the power and mystery of a life-affirming religion at work. Carefully explored with our students, the freedom struggle—most obviously in its southern manifestations—not only provides us all an entry point to the world of Black religion in the United States (an important and deeply moving subject in itself), but also demonstrate some of the ways in which the humanizing force of any religion can draw to its side valuable companions from other religious traditions." (Vincent Harding, scholar in the field of religion and social transformation, freedom activist, senior academic consultant to the award-winning PBS television series, *Eyes on the Prize*)

Invocation

As we enter into the gates of thanksgiving and praise, we call on you, gracious God, the Transformer of all life, the Liberator of all liberators, whom we come to praise, by grace in freedom, for the transformation of our lives and those we hope to minister to. Let us worship our God of freedom!

Reflections

In freedom, God creates us and invites us to an openness of faith as we seek to know liberation, praying to transcend vengeance and embrace deliverance. Building on faith, we are invited to experience freedom as the witness of God. In freedom, we have opportunities to help facilitate the healing of wounded hearts, bodies, minds, souls. Freedom is a precious gift that many have never known. Freedom, a component of God's grace, is so amazing, revitalizing, strengthening. The gift of freedom provides the place for creating a cornucopia of blessing. Freedom, the state or quality of being free, involves the absence of coercion, need, or constraint in choice or action. Freedom means one is not bound to another in slavery, in involuntary restraint, or because of another's power. To be free is to be independent, to be able to speak openly and frankly, to experience liberty. Freedom is costly, as it requires one to be responsible. When we are truly free, we have no need to be indifferent, to feel inferior or ugly. Embodied freedom is a release from needing to feel prejudiced or superior. Freedom emerges from the very core of our being. Freedom accords a sense of self that is noble and just, that wants to share and replicate itself.

Prayer

O God of freedom and hope, we thank you for the opportunity to live a faithful life of freedom. As we experience this gift of liberation, we know an incredible life with God, knowing that God cares for us, loves us in freedom, and has given us the gift of freedom to make decisions, discerning the difference between right and wrong. We embrace the blessing of freedom, a component of faith. We pray for men, women, and children over the world to have a life where freedom is foundational faith. We rejoice that we know God gives the gift of freedom, even when some human beings make choices and do things that blight this precious spiritual endowment. The experience of freedom is essential to healing. Healing cannot happen unless one chooses to be well and whole and free. Even if one is incarcerated, one can be free in spirit and in mind. Many who will never be behind bars are enslaved by circumstances, by misplaced desires, by a life where serenity is never attained.

Freedom allows us to admit our mistakes and name the harm we do. After naming this harm, one can then experience and express the depths of the accompanying pain and begin the healing process, while experiencing freedom in new ways. In the process, we come to see that each of us has value and is made in the image of God. In honoring this divine image, we come to know true freedom.

Litany

Leader: The eloquence of divinely given freedom provides stability for times when our insecurities and lack of confidence trap us into what others think, into what others do, into what others feel, or into what others agree on about what we must feel.

People: **For freedom, shaped by covenant joy and hope, we give thanks and are moved by God's generosity.**

Leader: Amid the turmoil we perceive in our lives, we know the blessing of our freedom, which provides opportunities for celebrating our health and well-being.

People: **The covenantal power of freedom reminds us that we are sacred, called to be good stewards as we share our experiences of liberation.**

Leader: As recipients of incarnated generosity, we embrace our freedom fully, completely, and remain committed to work for the cause of freedom.

People: **Majestic Sweetness, Loving Grace, in the gift of freedom we know comfort and offer profound gratitude to you. Thanks to your grace and love, we know that we are changing and that others can be changed, too.**

Benediction

As the bells toll for freedom, throughout the air, in our hearts and spirits, we go forth to share the message of liberation, how grace can set the captive free, how spiritual freedom grants us the peace that surpasses all knowledge and understanding. Go and tell this good news, that our Creator has endowed us with freedom, peace, and serenity, for all eternity. God be with you always; go now in peace. Amen.

—ᴠᴠ—

6. Health

Beloved, I pray that all may go well with you and that you may be in health; I know that it is well with your soul.
—3 John 1:2

Quotation

Health is not simply the absence of disease—it comprises a wide range of activities that foster healing and wholeness. . . . Health is a cultural production in that health and illness alike are social constructs and dependent on social networks, biology, and environment. As it is embedded in our social realities, health also includes the integration of the spiritual (how we relate to God), the mental (who we are as thinking and feeling people), and the physical (who we are biologically) aspects of our lives. . . . It is important to note that everything we do is mediated by our bodies. Part of the dilemma the Christian community faces when addressing health care is rooted in a negative dualism that separates the body and the spirit." (Emilie Townes, professor, preacher, scholar, author)

Invocation

As we stand in God's sanctuary, readying ourselves for praise and worship, we open ourselves to God, for God will bring health and healing, joy and comfort as we gather and open ourselves to the glory, mercy, and power of God.

Reflections

Whether the economy goes up or down, whether we are male or female, young or old, red, black, brown, yellow, or white in pigmentation, we all share the need to be healthy. Health is always essential in our lives. As we grow in faith and grace, we have the room to make a serious analysis of the past, assess the present, and make room for understanding ourselves. The more we appreciate who God has created us to be, the better able we are to hear a prophetic voice regarding the future. Faith challenges us and helps us meet the formidable tasks of life. Faith pushes us to be honest with ourselves about what we feel, think, and want. The more we love and nurture ourselves, the more we are pushed to examine our strengths and our weaknesses, particularly noting personal responsibility and accountability. We can begin to have the courage to face issues that seem almost impossible to comprehend and alter. God gives us the energy to believe that by grace, we are bigger than our issues and difficulties. Loving ourselves is not about being narcissistic or egocentric, but rather it is about being more appreciative of the gift of ourselves. The more self-esteem or self-worth we enjoy, the more healthy we are, and the more available we are to the abundance of Spirit.

Prayer

Healing and infinite presence, we thank you this day that every moment of our lives is blessing and possibility. You have blessed us with health and strength. When we are weak, you make us strong. In our coming and our going, in our work and our leisure time, we experience the gift of health. As your children, we are dynamic, living beings. You are ever steadfast and sure as you embrace change, as you embrace us. No matter the difficulty, help us never lose hope. Please temper our negative behavior patterns and help us ward off sick thinking, which causes impaired health. Bless us so that we never take our health for granted. Let us never assume that illnesses indicate sin or punishment. When we are sick and tired, touch our parched lips with the cool breath of kindness and consideration. Bless us so that we do not become sick in spirit, and help us see our health as a resource. Help us see the various interconnections amid our faith, health, and spirituality. Show us how to live in healthy, rewarding ways, working toward wellness and letting us be inspirational for others.

Litany

Leader: By God's grace, as we look in the mirror, we see ourselves; as we focus, we see God, love signified, and the beauty of God's healing and health in us.

People: **Sometimes we do not see our beauty, our strength given by God. We come to release our jaded attitudes and bask in gratitude for health and strength.**

Leader: When our anger and lack of confidence colors our vision and blurs our perception, help us appreciate what and how our bodies function.

People: **When our souls rejoice or when we need to wail, teach us that we are yours, that no pains are so cavernous, so deep, that spiritual amnesia need embrace us.**

Leader: When we take your beloved voice for granted, when we have illness and distress, still our hearts and our anxieties, that we may know your covenant love and forgiveness.

People: We sing with joy, as your mercy has painted over old jealousies, aches, and depressions, to make us new creatures in Christ Jesus, celebrating the gift of health and life.

Benediction

Rejoice, rejoice, go in peace! Serve God with gladness, honoring your bodies, minds, and spirits as sacred vessels of God, supporting us on the adventure of life. Go now in peace, committed to life habits that support and protect your health. God be with you always; go now in peace. Amen.

—∭—

7. Heritage/Culture

"No weapon that is fashioned against you shall prosper, /and you shall confute every tongue that rises against you in judgment. /This is the heritage of the servants of the LORD /and their vindication from me, says the LORD."
—Isaiah 54:17

Quotation

The lesson of history that all human rights are indivisible and that the failure to adhere to this principle jeopardizes the rights of all is particularly applicable here. A built-in hazard of an aggressive ethnocentric movement which disregards the interests of other disadvantaged groups is that it will become parochial and ultimately self-defeating in the face of hostile reactions, dwindling allies, and mounting frustrations." (Pauli Murray [1910–1985] feminist, lawyer, Episcopal priest)

Invocation

Glorious God of our ancestors, we proclaim your awesomeness and creative generosity in giving us families, heritages, and culture. In honor of these gifts, let us worship God!

Reflections

A life of sacredness is a life of willingness. This willingness includes the ability to love one's self, one's culture and heritage. Part of who we are concerns our sociohistorical contexts, our DNA, and our socialization as children. Some of us shun our culture and try to "pass" or slide into another class or cultural echelon, so that we do not have to identify with "those po' folk." To experience holistic salvation, we need to love and like ourselves, appreciate where we come from, and embrace our heritage. If unfortunate things happen to us because of our cultural heritage, we still need an awareness of self, culture, and our history. As we learn the story of our biblical and human ancestors, we can better make our own contributions; we can grow, willing to be changed, and willing to help change ourselves and our communities to create a viable, healthy society. To create dynamic, healthy cultural communities, we must be willing to be molded, reshaped, renewed. We need to be willing to see what is going on and then have the courage to congratulate and commend, to correct and admonish, and to name sick behavior and take actions to assure that it does not continue. Too often we claim something is not our business, or we play the victim. Dealing with victimhood may not be pleasant, but the unpleasantness does not give us license to look the other way; the stability of our cultural heritage is at stake. God's grace, corporate love, spiritually based social action, and knowledge of our history and heritage can make a difference.

Prayer

With a thousand tongues we sing praise to you in joyful thanksgiving for our color, our race, our history, and our ethnic culture.

29

We yield ourselves to your holiness and redemptive grace. In prayerful hope and faith, we offer thanks for your creative wisdom: you created your children in so many colors and gave us so many different experiences within our culture. We desire an intimacy with you that knows no boundaries, so that our own culture and the cultures of others will become a thing of value rather than a stumbling block. We crave your nearness. We need you in the healing of old wounds that worked to wipe out the honor of our cultural heritage. We give you thanks for the realization of new visions. Help us live, walk, and talk in a pathway of fairness that shuns revenge and vengeance, and that celebrates our heritage. Help us put our lives and heritage in a divine perspective as we live out our salvation in freedom, hope, and certainty. We bless you that this divine freedom enables us to celebrate our heritage and culture as gifts from you. Keep us close to you, beloved God, that we may release the enslavement of the past. In return, we will work as a community to not become enslaved to things, fame, money, or the expectations of others or of ourselves. We seek your counsel as we honor our blessed cultural heritage.

Litany

Leader: Who we are, and whose we are signals the power of God: we are divinely ordained, resilient, creative people with different cultural backgrounds.

People: **Because God makes our rich cultures and heritages possible, we rejoice for those who are willing to express themselves, risking bad choices, mistakes, or errors in judgment.**

Leader: Our cultures provide opportunities to tell stories about our ancestors and about our sisters and our brothers, stories which fuel hopeful transformation.

People: **Many are the tapestries, the different languages and dialects, the varieties of foods and drink that** arise from the particular way in which our cultures and heritages have functioned over many, many ages.

Leader: We give thanks that God has allowed us to create diverse ways to do family and to offer hospitality. We give thanks for the many different kinds of food, and arts and crafts, all of which are expressions of our God.

People: Our languages, our music, our folk sayings provide us with a strong sense of self-identity, unencumbered by those who seek to kill us as we leave a great cultural legacy to the world.

Benediction

As we honor the gifts of many generations and those many thousands gone who left behind no kindred or descendants, we go forth to live this day and give witness to the legacy of our ancestors and the holy legacy of Christ as we are blessed to become a blessing! God be with you always; go now in peace. Amen.

8. Laughter

For everything there is a season, and a time for every matter
under heaven: . . . a time to weep, and a time to laugh;
/a time to mourn, and a time to dance.
—Ecclesiastes 3:1, 4

Quotation

L aughter isn't even the other side of tears. It is tears turned inside out. Truly suffering is great here on earth. We blunder along, shredded by our mistakes, bludgeoned by our faults. Not having a clue where the dark path leads us. But on the whole, we stumble along bravely, don't you think?" (Alice Walker, Civil Rights activist, teacher, poet, novelist, writer, founder of Wild Tree Press)

Invocation

O blessed joyful souls, let us come to celebrate God as God laughs with us, honoring pure joy and renewal, refreshment, and restoration. Let us worship God!

Reflections

Laughter is an experience of showing mirth, joy, or scorn with a smile and chuckle or explosive sound. When we laugh we usually find pleasure or amusement about something. Sometimes we laugh out of unmitigated cheerfulness, joy, and gladness. Our laughter may be an indicator of human happiness and great delight. Sometimes we laugh nervously when we do not know what to say or do. One could imagine that God enjoys our laughter as much as we do. Several instances of joy in the biblical text are accompanied by laughter. For example, in prayers and songs for deliverance, one desires to hear joy and gladness in the midst of moral renewal (Psalm 51:8) and salvific deliverance (Isaiah 12:3). One knows joy when coming out of oppression, as seen in the Exodus and in returning from the exile (Isaiah 35:10; Jeremiah 31:13). Circumstances do not have to impede one's experience of joy. At the same time, amid devastation and loss, joy may wither away (Joel 1:12). In some texts, one circles in joy, rejoicing greatly and exceedingly in response to God's works and attributes. In the midst of vindication and healing, one goes to God's altar in praise and exceeding joy (Psalm 43:1-4). When we have been sad, and someone does something to relieve that feeling, we sometimes laugh. What a blessing to be able to laugh. When something is so funny that we cry and laugh at the same time, we know sheer gladness and delight. Laughter—what an awesome gift from God.

Prayer

God of grace and humor, we give thanks for the gift of laughter, which expresses life and brings joy and relaxation. How joyous that as we laugh, it is infectious, allowing others to know this gift of sacred joy and cheer. We pray for discernment, for laughter can be empowering and lead toward well-being; laughter can also be cruel and brutal when we laugh at people to embarrass and hurt them. We praise you through laughter and take such delight as we hear the gurgling laughter of children and the low chuckles of our seniors. Bless us to know that the joyful noise of laughter can be an act of praise. Help us to be attentive about how we respond to each other, that, by grace, our response will be appropriate and life giving. Help us to be grateful for the speech and hearing centers in our body that allow us to laugh and to hear the laughter of others. Help us daily find situations wherein we can laugh, dispelling the tensions that develop during the course of our days. For laughter, for tears of joy, for the healthy ways in which we have fun, we give thanks.

Litany

Leader: Great is God, and so are God's people; we lift our voices in speech, song, and laughter, knowing the gift of God's power through honoring communication, words, and sound, with every breath praising God.

People: **How awesome is our Creator God, who rejoices and laughs with us, for the strengthening of our whole selves and our relationships.**

Leader: How faithful are you, gracious God, through all generations; you have turned our mourning into laughter and dancing that overcomes oppression; you have turned our doubts into beliefs, and our separateness into unity.

People: **Blessed Healer, your faith inspires us to be faithful, loving, and laughing communities. The gift and medicine of laughter healed our ancestors, and keeps us well through difficulties and triumphs.**

Leader: In thanksgiving, we come praising you, to please and laugh with you, for only through your Grace can we experience you. Your blessing of salvation and healing with laughter brings us to freedom and peace.

People: **Throughout historical and present time, your gift of laughter has made us whole. Laughter provides a release, a new perspective, and a sense of renewal in hard times, and an experience of pure joy at times of blessing. For these gifts, we give thanks.**

Benediction

Friends, the news of the gospel is so good. Let us remember to laugh and share that gift of healing power as we leave here and go out to share the beauty and joy of God. God be with you always; go now in peace. Amen.

9. Recreation/Play

"And the streets of the city shall be full of boys
and girls playing in its streets."
—Zechariah 8:5

Quotation

My motto was always to keep swinging [playing]. Whether I was in a slump or feeling badly or having trouble off the field, the only thing to do was keep swinging." (Henry [Hank] Aaron, corporate vice president, with a 23-year Major League baseball career)

Invocation

Rejoice, rejoice, O people of God, as we enter into a time and a space of joy and thanksgiving, a place where we can play in the Spirit, as we are open to being recreated! Let us worship God!

Reflections

To many of us, the concept of play is an experience relegated only to the very young. When we limit play in this way, however, we shortchange our own experience of life and the many blessings of God. Adults need to play just as children do. When we engage in play, we use our imagination; we visualize outside of the standard way of contemplation. Being open to play gives us opportunities to relax, to reduce stress, and to experience renewal. Many of us take ourselves much too seriously. We worry so much that we lose our joy, our resilience, our sense of balance. When we lose our sense of balance, our physical, spiritual, and emotional health can be hampered. To lose a sense of playfulness can thwart our creativity and our ability to be spontaneous. Many people engage in play by being a spectator. Some people enjoy professional and amateur sports; some play board games; some take exercise classes. Many attend the events of friends, children, and grandchildren to cheer them on. Reading, dabbling in art, going to museums, taking walks, singing favorite songs on a trip or around the piano, playing chess, and attending retreats are all ways in which we can play, have fun, and take time to recreate ourselves and recharge ourselves.

Prayer

Marvelous God, we give thanks for the time to recreate and enjoy being with others. We are so blessed to be able to use our minds, bodies, and spirits in lighthearted ways. The ability to enjoy ourselves and others, and to focus on being together without having to take care of business, is one way that you help us restore our soul. How blessed are we that you have created us to be many faceted creatures who have the capacity to imagine and play and enjoy humor. Thank you for honoring and blessing us by giving us humor, enjoyment, and satisfaction. We pray that we never use our humor and play to ridicule, to make fun of another, or to engage in cruelty. We ask for guidance in helping those who are so serious and bitter, that their ability to play is severely hampered. Help us experience relaxation as we play, so that we do not confuse recreation with competition. We honor you by taking time to play. We honor ourselves by understanding that playing is a valuable, important part of our lives. Help us not be afraid of experiencing recreation, for play can help transform our lives.

Litany

Leader: We make a joyful noise, and we delight in laughter and playful imagination that helps us to rejuvenate ourselves, to honor creation, honor God, and focus on what is important.

People: The joy of playing and having fun is a spiritual gift
          that is available for us daily. We give thanks for the
          gift of play, and pray that we will exercise and find
          value in this gift.

Leader: O magnify our God, who created us with the gifts of
          laughter and of having fun. May we honor God by
          engaging in play that is healthy and brings about
          peace.

People: When stressful days come, may we remember to
          run, or clap, or dance, or read, or color, or take out
          a board game, to help us release that which is creat-
          ing stress until we are able to cope from a place of
          strength.

Leader: O playful God, did you not use your largest artistic
          palette, greatest sense of humor, most creative imagi-
          nation when you fashioned us and shaped the world?

People: In this moment, we elevate our hands and open our
          hearts to hear the good news of the gospel pro-
          claimed as we participate in playing. Hallelujah, hal-
          lelujah, hallelujah.

Benediction

As we leave to go out and do the Jesus stuff, let us be ever mindful of the gift of play, and may we remember that there is a time
and place for everything. God be with you always; go now in
peace. Amen.

10. Funerals

My lyre is turned to mourning, and my pipe to
the voice of those who weep.
—Job 30:31

Quotation

The funeral is a critical ritual in the African American community. It is a time of gathering family, solace, sermon, and song; a time of humor and food. It is a time when the church and community family becomes enmeshed with the immediate family. As eighty-year-old Miss Eliza sat in her rocking chair, selecting scriptures from the 'frayed family Bible,' deciding on flowers, humming 'Just a Closer Walk with Thee,' coordinating her burial outfit, and deciding who would sit with Melissa—her only family—Melissa covertly drank away the pain of losing her grandmother." (Teresa L. Fry Brown, professor, minister, author)

Invocation

Gathered at this hour, we come before your presence with humble heart, witnessing to the lives of loved ones who have joined the ancestral chorus. Let us worship God!

Reflections

Funerals are the observances held for a dead person usually before burial or after cremation. Many people also have memorial services, which usually occur after the funeral and the disposition of the body. The funeral, a form of worship service, honors and eulogizes the dead. Depending upon the particular tradition, the funeral may be a service that is quiet and brief. The service may be a celebration and time of honoring an individual's home-going. Sometimes the funeral service is known as a celebration of the resurrection of the deceased. When people have been ill for an extended period of time or when they are older, death and thus funerals are not unexpected. Whether a death is expected or a sudden tragedy, we tend not to handle death and its related rituals too well. Premature deaths due to illness, accidents, or foul play are most difficult for many of us to reconcile. The role of the church family, friends, and clergy is to honor the deceased and provide comfort for those who mourn. There are many uncertainties in life, and knowing that from the day when you were born, you began to die does not lessen the severity of grief. Yet, we can live each day in joy and peace, honoring differences, listening well, and spending time with family, so that when death comes there will be no regrets. "Live each day as if you would live forever, but live each day as if it were your last" (*Zorba, the Greek*).

Prayer

Comforting, loving God, we thank you for life itself, and the life of our beloved friend and family member whom we now mourn. Give us the strength to see the most in each other as we grieve together, that we might not spend disproportionate time in dealing with regrets, mistakes, and disappointments, but that we would recall the joyful, fulfilling, and loving times we shared with our departed loved one. Help us find heightened meaning in life. Help those who are on their deathbeds to embrace your Light in thanksgiving for their gift of life. Help their caregivers to treat those who are dying with utmost dignity and respect, honoring their wishes for a good death. Please be with those who mourn, those who remain in deep pain. When lives have been cut short, help the family and colleagues who mourn, and help us not pressure them to "just get over it." Realizing that many deaths are unexpected, give us all a spirit of compassion, so that we can walk beside those who grieve. Give us words, your words of assurance, so that families can take time to mourn, not being trapped in the mournful process or in denial. Blessed One, give us a garment of peace and comfort as we mourn, that one day, we will be at peace.

Litany

Leader: This is the day of new life in Christ Jesus, even as we mourn and bury our dead; be with us, that we might experience grace amid our troubled, burdened spirits.

People: **In this hour of grief, when pain seems unspeakable, we long, O God, for your presence and your mercy. Thank you for the life of our loved one, who blessed us.**

Leader: This is the hour of mourning and deep pain; yet we know that you have promised never to forsake us or leave us alone. We give thanks for your comfort.

People: **In this moment of our anguish, we are so grateful for friends and other family members who stand beside us, holding us, with our faulty steps and breaking hearts.**

Leader: This is the experience that we will all have to take; as we walk with the mourning, we realize that, one day, we too will be mourned. Fit us now for the living, and help us be there for the dying.

People: **May we all see life as gift, and not fear death. May we live and contribute in each moment, so that when death comes we have no regrets, only hope and a sense of accomplishment and peace.**

Benediction

As Ecclesiastes people, who know we have a time to live and a time to die, a time to weep and a time to mourn, bless us as we leave here, that we might live life and live it abundantly, in gratitude and in peace. God be with you always; go now in peace. Amen.

11. Marriage

Jesus also was invited to the marriage, with his disciples.
—John 2:2

Quotation

We have shifted from an understanding of marriage as religious and communal to regarding it as legal and social. I know that people continue to have church weddings. This does not mean, however, that marriage is still held to be sacred. . . . Spiritual obligation tends to be the furthest thing from the couple's mind. People continue to associate the ceremony with the church although they have separated spirituality from marriage. . . . Couples will take months to plan a wedding but not think about marriage until after the legal document has been signed." (Lee H. Butler Jr., Baptist minister, professor, pastoral care counselor)

Invocation

Families and friends and partners and spouses, let us come to honor God as we gather, honoring the sanctity of marriage and the gifts of all relationships! Let us worship God!

Reflections

Marriages do not happen by magic, and the wedding ceremonies are not the pinnacle of the marriage. The wedding ceremony only unlocks the door. Some people are in love with being in love rather than with their spouse. They think that once the vows have been said, the cake has been cut, and thank-you notes have been sent, they can change the person they married. Ultimately, only God can help us change, if we are open to it. The marriage license is a public, legal record of a spiritual, God-given commitment. Marriage requires work and deep faithfulness. Marriage concerns establishing a covenantal relationship. A covenant is an agreement or compact between two parties binding them mutually to endeavors on each other's behalf. Theologically, this compact pertains to a gracious undertaking entered into by God for the benefit and blessing of humanity. To grow a healthy covenantal marriage, both parties must seek out God as the Author of the marriage and the Giver of the most helpful, healthy, loving partner for marriage. In a covenantal marriage, both parties feel they are connected by a spiritual force for deep commitment, which depends upon healthy communications, learning to ask the right questions of God and our partner, listening well, and then carrying out the indicated mutually beneficial actions. In a covenantal marriage, each party allows the other to grow at his or her own rate, mutually supports the other, takes pride in his or her accomplishments, is sexually intimate, enjoys the other's company, makes the relationship a high priority, and prayerfully stands by the other partner through good times and bad, limiting blame and judgment. A covenantal marriage is a consummate friendship. Actions of prayer and seeking wise counsel need to be followed with listening, confessing, releasing, forgiving, and loving. Some of us are legally married to a person, but in reality we are married to our work. Parties must understand that the marriage is a divine call by God. With God as head of the family, daily restoration of the covenantal commitment strengthens the love. With compassionate love comes a new kind of knowledge, revelation, and manifestation of our own new sacred relationship: a true covenantal marriage.

Prayer

Loving God, we pray for all marriages, for all engaged couples, for all of those in close relationships who may be contemplating or seeking long-term commitments. Bless us to respect each individual within this two-party relationship made in your divine image. Teach us to counsel and nurture couples to understand that before saying "I do," each party needs prayerfully to discern whether you are calling them to this marriage. If not, help the couple garner the courage not to get married. Help us have a divinely ordained way of knowing how to proceed when thinking about making a life-long commitment to another. Bless the friends and family of the couple so that they may know when to comment and when to keep a respectful silence and distance. Bless all those who take authority to marry persons. Enable each couple to partake of premarital counseling, so that their relationship can flourish. Help long-married couples take time to continue to grow and nurture their relationship and each other. In instances of domestic violence, protect those who are victimized, convert, where possible, the hearts of the perpetrators, and enable society to put an end to the evils of emotional, spiritual, and physical abuse of partner and family.

Litany

Leader: We rise amid our collective history, that which has formed us—the great rewards and the massive disappointments; we bring all of these experiences to a marriage as we seek to experience covenant together.

People: **From the rising to the setting of the sun, from the rising moments in our lives to the setting satisfaction of our accomplishments, we live amid hurt, frustrations, and mistakes in marriage. A God-ordained covenantal marriage survives still.**

Leader: As the light of God radiates throughout our lives, God calls us to marriages of liberation: God gives us the freedom to be individuals, as well as one flesh;

43

God is the head, and the two persons are equally
yoked partners.

People: **For blessings of marriage, covenant love, and
patience, we give thanks; we affirm our covenant
relationship with God, incarnated in our lives as
together we live, make love, and know joy.**

Leader: When we are troubled in our marriage, we call on the
Lord; when we are angry beyond control, we cry out
to the One who hears our cry, cherishes our thoughts,
and wants to help us heal.

People: **As we dwell as two and one on earth, and as you
dwell on earth and in heaven, we magnify you,
rededicating our marriage as a blessing to you, the
One who gives us resilience, righteousness, resurrection, and hope.**

Benediction

As bells ring of joy, birdseed is thrown, doves are released, and
the last tones of the organ quiet, let us go in peace honoring the
sanctity of marriage and of life commitments to the glory of God.
God be with you always; go now in peace. Amen.

—m—

12. Reunions

*Let us not give up meeting together, as some are in the habit of doing,
but let us encourage one another—and all the more
as you see the Day approaching.*
—Hebrews 10:25 (NIV)

Quotation

The family reunion movement cultivates pride of heritage. It brings persons in an extended family network together in times of joy as well as sorrow. . . . It is an intergenerational gathering. . . . [There is] a caring and sharing spirit that spills over into ongoing relationships between cousins and extended family. . . . We cannot take this movement for granted, and we are grateful for it. It has brought great benefits to black family life." (J. Deotis Roberts, professor, author)

Invocation

Rejoice, for the day is here when we honor our ancestors, our families, and our extended families. We honor our legacy of hope in anticipation of a blessed today and a promising future. Let us worship God.

Reflections

Families are peculiar sometimes. This connection of relatives can be such a blessing and joy, but they can also "get on our last nerve." At its best, families are an integral part of life. We are grateful for knowing that we have relatives, that connections have been made before our birth, and it is these connections of bloodline and biology, of adoption and extended family that we come to rejoice. Reunions have multiplied in recent years. After the televising of Alex Haley's *Roots*, many people recognized that we ought not to take family for granted and that families and the times we have shared together are important. During family reunions we learn the stories about our parents and grandparents. We see other folk who look and act just like we do: our noses and flat feet, our hips and big, beautiful eyes, our funny laughs and the way we talk with our hands, our particular talents, our love of God and gift of voice. Reunions are times of discovery and recovery; we meet relatives we never knew before. When we return home, we feel renewed, complete, and blessed, simply because we are family.

Prayer

Creator God, give us clean hearts, open minds, and loving spirits as we reunite with family and friends from across the land. Help us mold our family *[or organization name, or class]* into a viable, healthy community. Where we do not have healthy families *[organizations, schools]*, help us find faith communities and other people who will make up our extended family. Help us love those who have caused us harm, but let us not become their victim, someone they can disrespect. As we experience this reunion, help us develop a sense of values that affirm the godliness within us, fostering renewal and hope in our communities. Bless us with the wisdom of knowing the significance of our lives, our families *[organizations]*, and the ministries we are called to in our church and local communities. Let this reunion be an exquisite example of community building and collaboration. As we remember you, please remember us *[or organization name or class and year]*. Deliver us from wrongdoing and self-destruction; reunite us with family and friends, forever and always.

Litany

Leader: We bless you God, for our ancestors and kin, for friends and loved ones who make up our family. We are grateful for that sense of belonging, of sameness, of difference within us.

People: **Blest be the tie of family that binds us together. We honor and salute togetherness, even in the difficult times, which let us grow in love.**

Leader: We bless each other for the gift of self, of sharing, of loving because we are connected by blood, by adoption, because we care.

People: **Blest be the tie of family that binds us together. We honor all adopted and extended family members. We**

have chosen you, and you are so special to us; we
extend the title of family to you.

Leader: We bless our ancestors for being who they were. We
give thanks for the gift of life and pray for those who
have tried but have not been blessed with biological
family. We pray for all families who experience abuse,
that they might stop the behavior, get counseling, and
find family who can love them well.

People: **Blest be the tie of family that binds us together. We
honor all people, all kinds of families and extended
families, praying that each family see life in family
as a privilege.**

Benediction

We rejoice that we have had the time to celebrate family. May
we go in joy and hope, honoring family, and friends who make
up family. May we love and respect all people, for everyone needs
to belong. God be with you always; go now in peace. Amen.

13. Sacraments (Sacred Rites)

*"These are the appointed feasts of the LORD, the holy [sacred] convoca-
tions, which you shall proclaim at the time appointed for them."*
—Leviticus 23:4

Quotation

The African (Babukusu) rites of birth and naming have
several similarities with Christian infant baptism. First of
all, the African Rites mark the passage of the child into

this world and the young mother from girlhood to motherhood, whereas Christian baptism celebrates passage into the new life of Christ. Second, the African Rites incorporate the individual into the clan and the community of adults, and the Christian rites welcomes the initiate (child) into the church, the People of God, the community of believers." (Anne Nasimiyu-Wasike, Kenyan religious sister, professor)

Invocation

Children of God, rejoice as we enter into this sacred place, making a sacrament of this worship service where we join as the Body of Christ to adore our Creator, Redeemer, Sustainer: Let us worship God!

Reflections

That the God of covenant cares, loves justice and mercy, and is involved in the daily lives of believers is most clear in the biblical text. The importance of covenant embodied in meals and rituals is present in the Gospels in Jesus' baptism and in the Last Supper. We celebrate the connectedness between God and the children of Israel and the renewal and restatement of this connection through the Christ event (birth, life, death, and resurrection of Jesus Christ) in the Lord's Supper or the Eucharist. We celebrate baptism as an initiation rite. While some denominations have more sacraments, most revere the Eucharist (also known as the Lord's Supper or Communion) and baptism (whether solemnized at birth or as a confirmation of belief). A sacrament is an outward symbol, a visible manifestation of God's covenant promise and of our dedication to God. Sacraments invoke intimacy, care, nurture, and a delight of God in humanity and humanity in God: sacraments provide a setting, an environment for forging personal and communal inclusiveness, peace, and healthy, holistic spirituality.

Prayer

Beneficent God, in you we celebrate a life of holiness that embraces a life of responsibility, and we remember your goodness as we partake of the sacraments. From our dependence on you, we have the strength and courage to live life fully, remembering life's holiness as we recall the sacred rituals of baptism and Eucharist. Even during our wilderness experiences, the grace, symbolized in these sacraments, brings us respite in an oasis. Yet, in many parts of the world, there is little peace, the oases seem to be nonexistent, and we tend to forget the mystical, sacred nature and nurture of the meal prepared by Jesus of Nazareth. As we partake of these sacraments, help us experience your presence in a time of oasis for ourselves and others. Bless us to honor these sacraments and to be open to experience them anew each time. We give thanks that the sacraments are an opportunity for us to worship as an organic community in relationship. As one is baptized, we share a rite of passage into a new loving life in Christ Jesus. When partaking of the sacraments, we remember Jesus' words: "my yoke is easy and my burden is light" (Matthew 11:30). We give witness to the light, as the ability to see. We give thanks that as sight triggers responsibility, we will know that responsibility as an honor and not a burden.

Litany

Leader: Precious God, our Strength, our Redeemer, you are so generous! We praise your benevolence as we participate in the sacraments.

People: **Powerful God, our Hope, our Guide, because you have been present for us for all generations, we give thanks. We desire to model your integrity and uprightness by faith through your grace, celebrated in the sacraments.**

Leader: Precious Lord, who sustains us in times of great joy and in the agony of quiet despair; continue to be with us as we take the bread and the cup.

People: Loving God, Midwife and Architect of the world, we celebrate that you hear our prayers, especially as we welcome others to our community through the sacrament of baptism.

Leader: Magnificent weaver of all life, your beauty permeates all of creation. Refresh us with the fruit of your love that we may better appreciate all life, and our communities, as we partake of your blessed sacraments.

People: Majestic Potter, who sculpts our lives and all reality, we are the clay so marvelously made by you. Make us and mold us to the glory of your witness on earth. Let us know you as we stand at the table and before the altar in prayer.

Benediction

Most holy sacred God, as we depart to serve, to proclaim the sacredness of your creation, grant us your magnificent peace, that we may treat all with respect and dignity, embracing difference and focusing on you. God be with you always; go now in peace. Amen.

14. Worship

And Ezra said: "Thou art the LORD, thou alone; thou hast made heaven, the heaven of heavens, with all their host, the earth and all that is on it, the seas and all that is in them; and thou preservest all of them; and the host of heaven worships thee."
—Nehemiah 9:6

Quotation

Thus the peculiar social history of Black people and the dynamics of Black religious faith . . . have produced an amalgam of religious experience . . . in Black worship, there exists three primary support systems, preaching, praying, and singing. . . . Preaching: the heart of Black worship. . . . The preaching and theology of Black preachers with all the imperfections, gave cohesion and commonality to an oppressed people. . . . Praying: the strength of Black worship. . . . [P]rayer is the act of lifting one's consciousness to God in some physical and/or verbal manner whose end is to blend the worshipper's will with that of the omnipotent God. It (praying) is the means by which we 'talk' with God. . . . Singing: the Joy of Black worship. . . . [J]oy has to do with the posture of the soul and the spirit . . . joy is of the Lord and it can be triggered by good or bad news. . . . The religious music of Black Christians was shaped in the crucible of slavery but it bespeaks the existentialist faith that was the linch-pin of our survival." (Wyatt Tee Walker, preacher, pastor, artist, businessman, peace activist)

Invocation

Welcome, all you saints of God. This is the moment that God has given us to engage in worship, renewal, healing, and hope! Let us worship God.

Reflections

The term *worship*, can be used in positive and negative ways. When one objectifies or commodifies a person, or gives undue reverence to an object, a human being, or a particular experience, this is idolatry. Scripture tells us that no one or nothing comes before God. Worship in the positive sense, is the action of offering God or a supernatural power praise and adoration. To worship God is to express deep reverence and honor. Many worship services include a time of religious practice involving creeds, particular belief systems, or forms of ritual. Worship services proper contain prayers, music and singing, scripture readings, offerings (financial gifts), the Eucharist (Lord's Supper or Communion), and the proclamation of the Word, the event of preaching. Corporate or communal worship is a time when the entire community comes together for nurture, support, and purpose. Daily private devotional experience can involve Bible study, inspirational readings, prayer, or meditation. For some, journaling or jogging is integral to their devotion. One needs to find time on a daily basis to receive spiritual nurture, discernment, and guidance. Being quiet and literally "naked" and undistracted before God can be the beginning for untold revelations and ease.

Prayer

Our souls cling to you, Dear Lord; we thirst for you, as we gather in your sanctuary. We go through the wildernesses of our lives, thirsting to be in your oasis of hope and strength. As we cling to you, we remember our covenant to worship you daily, in season and out of season, for you remember us in special ways. Help us worship and praise you in gratitude, so that our false pride cannot alienate us from you. Bless us to be open to the anointing of the Holy Spirit in service. As we worship you daily, help us have a healthy sense of self-esteem, and give us a community commitment to unity as we celebrate diversity. Please, let no harm come to us. You only are our God, and to you only do we pray. You are willing to hold our burdens and be with us as we contemplate making decisions about our lives: for this, we are humbled. In this humility, help us follow those spiritual disciplines that make us well, as individuals and in community. Guide us in learning how to pray, to meditate, to do the various exercises and rituals that connect us with you in health. Be always near us and help our souls be still that we may be fully present for you. May your nearness remind us to do justice, love mercy, and be in charity with our neighbors.

Litany

Leader: We come into God's presence, into the place consecrated for the worship of God, a place made sacred by the thousands of prayers and testimonies in the preached and shared words that have gone forth from inside these walls.

People: We desire to worship in spirit and truth, that we might have a clearer conscious awareness of God and God's plan for our lives.

Leader: In the most grand or simple vestments and robes, in suits and clean work-a-day clothing, we come to the Mount of Olives and to Mount Zion, our cities high on a hill, as we connect with God.

People: We desire to be made whole, as God would have us be. Thus, we come to worship, seeking renewal and assurance that God loves us still.

Leader: With music plain or complex; in English, Spanish, Latin, Swahili, or Greek; with the cultural backgrounds of Asia, Africa, Europe, and South and North Americas, we worship now.

People: We make a joyful noise unto God, as we sing and shout and, like David, dance, for the Lord is good, and God's mercy endures forever.

Benediction

Now that our time for worship is over, let us go forth, inspired, renewed, and excited as we depart to be disciples of the faith to those who are waiting to hear the gospel news! God be with you always; go now in peace. Amen.

15. Anger

But now put them all away: anger, wrath, malice, slander,
and foul talk from your mouth.
—Colossians 3:8

Quotation

But anger expressed and translated into action in the service of our vision and our future is a liberating and strengthening act of clarification; for it is in the painful process of this translation that we identify who are our allies with whom we have grave difference, and who are our genuine enemies." (Audre Lorde [1934–1992], author, poet, activist)

Invocation

Today is the most important day of our lives, as we come to a new awareness of the transformational power of anger used well. Let us worship with openness and discernment toward a renewal of life in joy and thanksgiving!

Reflections

Some of us are spiritually and emotionally blind, and we have no spiritual guide dog, Braille, or laser cane to help us see our anger or the anger in others. Our physical vision is good, and we function well, but we cannot, and in some instances do not, want to see our emotional selves. At some point, we were wounded, and we have been living with infected boils and lesions of anger ever since. Each day the abscesses get worse. Sometimes we are so mean and angry, so terrified at our own pathology, and in such denial, that we have to project our sickness onto others and make others uncomfortable as well. Such an illness tends to metastasize and wreak havoc when such persons are in offices of power, producing dysfunction bordering on insanity. Such angry persons are often so skilled at manipulating others, that those who work under them may protest to higher authorities, often to no avail. Only when all of us—leader and follower, parent and child, spouse and partner—confront our demons, especially those of anger, can we begin the healing process. Anger in and of itself is not bad; what we do with anger can be creative or destructive, life-giving, or death-making.

Prayer

Omnipotent God, Giver of all life, help us know ourselves so that we can see who we are and know what we feel. Help us acknowledge our anger and not be embarrassed or afraid. Help us see our strong feelings of displeasure and hostility, so that we can use them in creative, helpful ways. Sometimes our anger colors our vision and blurs our perception of your love. Sometimes we have been so hurt by family, friends, or associates that we are just a bundle of chaotic emotions. Our anger gets tangled with jealousy, envy, lust, and confusion. Our souls, no longer able to rejoice, simply cry out from the deep woundedness, old hurts, and cavernous pains until we are cloaked in emotional and spiritual amnesia. Because of your mercy and compassion, we know that we do not have to be the victims of our own emotional state. Help us focus on the sources of our pains, and help us return to our centers. Bless us to use our anger and sadness in creative venues to uplift ourselves and others. By grace, our old jealousies, ignorance, and depressions can become the colors to paint pictures for others, showing them how they can know peace and joy in you, our Comforter, our overcoming Helper.

Litany

Leader: Glory to God in the highest, the God who gives us life and a vast palette of emotions, including anger, which allows us to express and communicate.

People: **Blessed are we, the people of God, who have access to our many emotions. May we be fully aware of our strengths, weaknesses, and emotions—especially our anger. May we see, not deny, our anger, that we may use it responsibly.**

Leader: Anger can be a tool of creativity or a tool of destruction. May we use our anger to energize us as we live our lives amid the certainty of God and the uncertainty of what we may face during the course of the day.

People: **Anger is not an emotion to be feared, to be projected onto others, or to be denied or used as a weapon. Anger is an emotion that allows us to experience and register unease and discomfort.**

Leader: We give thanks for an ability to think and feel, to discern safety and danger, to live a responsible life in Christ Jesus, aware of our anger, and of how to use it for health and well-being.

People: **In faith and possibility, we accept responsibility for using our anger in creative ways. When we desire to use our anger for destructive purposes, may our covenant promise to love stop us from doing harm.**

Benediction

Amid the possibilities of life, to daily respond in joy or anger, may we go forth to love and be in relationship with our neighbors and ourselves in respectful, honorable ways. God be with you always; go now in peace. Amen.

—m—

16. Death

For I am sure that neither death, nor life, nor angels, nor principalities, nor things present, nor things to come, nor powers, nor height, nor depth, nor anything else in all creation, will be able to separate us from the love of God in Christ Jesus our Lord.
—Romans 8:38-39

Quotation

And what do I regret? Surely not that I stand in the knowledge of the presence of death. For knowledge is a good thing; you have said that. What I regret is that in the face of death and all that it is and all that it shall be I stand powerless, that in the face of death my will, to which everything I have ever known bends, stands as if it were nothing more than a string caught in the early-morning wind." (Jamaica Kincaid, author)

Invocation

As we enter into communion with God and ourselves, we invite the Holy Spirit, to anoint us with thanksgiving as we entertain eternity, that of life and of death, the two sides of our living reality with you. Let us worship God!

Reflections

In Gilbert and Sullivan's *Pirates of Penzance*, one of the rousing choruses speaks of "a most ingenious paradox." The orphan boy Frederic ostensibly is coming of legal age, for he has lived twenty-one years, but because he was born on February 29, technically he's just a little over five years old. Our experience of life and death, too, is like "a most ingenious paradox." Daily we live on continuums of choices; daily people die—sometimes expectedly, sometimes prematurely. We don't understand why babies die stillborn, why drunk drivers kill and often walk away without a scratch. We don't understand why apparently healthy, robust young adults die within hours from aneurysms. And even when our parents and grandparents have reached seventy, we still don't understand why they have to die so soon. Like Job, we ask questions and may never have the reasons. Amid God's creative chaos we call life, we stand at the crossroads of danger and redemption. Sometimes the gift of redemption is incredibly dangerous, particularly when a commitment to a salvific life means we will have to change who we thought we were and what we had been doing. Death is a part of life. We are called to live life daily, carefully, and abundantly. There are no excuses for death inflicted on others by acts of rage and violence. Much about our bodies even the foremost scientists do not yet understand. Some deaths occur because of hereditary diseases, some because of carelessness, and some because of violence. Whatever the cause, on the day you were born you began to die, and one day you *will* die. The question is how will we live in the in-between time.

Prayer

Shepherd and Keeper of all persons, we come, grateful but fearful, for we are often troubled and pained by death. We know that with life comes death, but we want to keep our loved ones with us, and it is so hard to let them go. We know we ought to be grateful for any moment of life, and we are grateful for this time. But often, the days pass too quickly. The end of life comes and we have not had the time to honor people who have been good to us. Sometimes we have made choices that we feel we have never overcome. Sometimes our choices have led us down paths others said we should take, and we therefore never fully came to your path for us. We know, O God, that you have made each of us wonderfully and uniquely. Sometimes we are so overwhelmed by your generosity that we really cannot believe you would bless us so. Help us fully appreciate life and not fear death. Bless us to see that death is but another cycle of life. We have seasons in our lives, and one of the seasons is death. Some of us do not fear death, but we fear dying. Help us embrace the mystery, the ambiguity of life and death. Help us make peace with ourselves and our loved ones long before our hour of death. Help us die easy, secure in your love and your gift of salvation.

Litany

Leader: Covenant God, we cry out for your help and aid in this time of change and crisis. Be our strength and our sanctuary as we worship you in spirit and truth.

People: **God of the displaced and of those who seek refuge, we come before you with respect and trembling, knowing that you care for all of your children. We come expressing gratitude for the experience of your sanctuary as we face death.**

Leader: Gracious God, lover of justice, purveyor of mercy, hear our prayer for peace and serenity. Hold us so that our focus in life and death will be on you.

People: **God of the homeless and the terminally ill, we know that you are Emmanuel. We know that you hold us, all of us—the destitute, the determined, the hopeful, the hurting, the young, and the old—close to you, from eternity to eternity.**

Leader: Gracious God, hear our prayers that we may be at peace; gird us up with your desires. Stretch out your arms to us and embrace us where we are, that we may grow to be who you created us to be, that we may die well.

People: **God of children, youth, and adults, God of those who are very intelligent, the average thinkers, and those who are mentally challenged, we give thanks for the ability to think, read, and know a fulfilled life. Help us embrace death so that we too, can say "well done."**

Benediction

Beloveds, you who daily face life, and sometimes face the death of others, as you go forth from our time of worship, go vowing to live life fully and embrace death as another phase of life. God be with you always; go now in peace. Amen.

—∿—

17. Disappointment

And hope does not disappoint us, because God's love has been poured into our hearts through the Holy Spirit which has been given to us.
—Romans 5:5

Quotation

All I know is most people's lives are a great disappointment to them and no one leaves this earth without feeling terrible pain. And if there is no divine explanation at the end of it all, well . . . that's sad." (Kasi Lemmons, actor, director, filmmaker)

Invocation

Most gracious God, we come to worship and be renewed; we lift up our disappointments and our desires as we come to be blessed. Let us worship God!

Reflections

Life is full of ups and downs, of joys and sorrows, of fulfilled dreams and of disappointments. To disappoint means to fail to meet the expectations or hopes of, to frustrate, or to baffle. One can be disappointed by another person or a situation; one can also disappoint others by failing to live up to their expectations, by committing acts that defraud, deceive, or cheat another. We disappoint others when we circumvent or avoid dealing with reality, or when we seek to foil, ruin, or thwart someone's plans. The Christian life calls us to live an ethical existence, one that values the good and respects all humanity. The other side of disappointment is when bad things happen to us or our community. When we lose jobs, when friends move away or die, we know tremendous grief and disappointment. We get frustrated when we have no control over the events that affect our lives. Disappointments are a part of life. This does not mean that we look for pain and problems, or that we set ourselves up to experience such trouble. Experiencing disappointment is an opportunity to reevaluate our level of expectations and the reasonableness of those expectations so that we do not create disappointing environments or communities around us.

Prayer

Counselor, merciful God, bless us as we go about our daily lives and experience disappointments, regrets, and misunderstandings. Help us create the kinds of communities that can affirm who we are and show us dignity and respect. When we enter into relationships, help us experience empathy, so that we can see how people experience us. Bless us to become more sensitive in our communication, so that we avoid giving mixed and confusing messages. Guard our tongues that they may be faithful tools of love and justice, not implements of scorn and hate. Teach us to be good stewards so that we will not overcommit ourselves and disappoint others. Help us understand how we can communicate in integrity and peace. When we are disappointed, help us name that pain. Help us navigate the many emotions that arise, the anxiety, sadness, grief, frustration, and loss that come with disappointment. Bless us so that we can learn more about who we are and what part, if any, we had in causing the circumstances that led to our feelings of confusion and disrespect. At eventide, bless us with peace and hopeful anticipation, grateful for the day that has just passed, optimistic for the day yet to come.

Litany

Leader: Bless the Lord. From the depths of our souls, we cry out as the ravages of disappointment dampen our ability to receive your grace, to confess our wrong, and confront the wrongs of others.

People: **Holy are you, who cares for us unceasingly as we falter in our covenantal relationship with you, our neighbors, and ourselves.**

Leader: Your magnificence is great, and it provides the love that can illumine our disappointments, working to show us the level of our own misguided expectations.

People: **Holiness is our birthright, as we are made in your image. May we live in this light in a way that lets us recognize our disappointments, but refuses to be defeated by them.**

Leader: What joy and peace we have knowing that you, O God, care about us, and even when you are disappointed in the way we live, you love us still.

People: **We give thanks, for each day is a new opportunity to accord others respect and dignity, lessening the possibility that we will cause disappointments beyond repair.**

Benediction

In the Name of the One who saves and cares for us, we leave this place to go forth hoping that we will not disappoint ourselves and others, but will honor the covenant of love God has set before us. God be with you always; go now in peace. Amen.

—ᴡᴡ—

18. Doubt

And Jesus answered them, "Truly, I say to you, if you have
faith and never doubt, you will not only do what has been
done to the fig tree, but even if you say to this mountain,
'Be taken up and cast into the sea,' it will be done."
—Matthew 21:21

Quotation

How can you go somewhere no one else has gone before? . . . they whispered. Their doubts gave me doubt. Their lack of faith tried to extinguish the flame God had started in my soul." (Sheron C. Patterson, pastor, author)

Invocation

As we enter into this holy sanctuary, into this consecrated space of hope, we put aside all doubts, giving them to God as we come to engage in praise, worship, and thanksgiving.

Reflections

A faithful life has an incredible amount of space for belief and doubt. Doubt concerns the state of uncertainty, of not being clear about what one believes. When one encounters doubt, one may hesitate in making decisions or taking specific action. Sometimes doubt leads to distrust or a lack of confidence. We tend to get most uncomfortable about our doubt when we feel something morally wrong about being unsure or questioning. Doubt can be healthy, a catalyst for attaining renewed, resurrected faith by God's grace. Sometimes encountering doubt begins new faith. A life that allows us to face doubt embodies a kind of illumination; if we but look, the light of faith may get us started on a helpful path. Doubt may be a good step for those of us who have gotten complacent and taken our faith for granted. A faithful life that has room for doubt spares us the insanity of desperation. Desperation repels, it does not attract. People do not like the pathological neediness that comes with desperation. Doubt can be refreshing, and it can allow us to name that which is good and that which needs to change. A faithful life that has room for doubt helps us stand on the edge of desolate places and see beyond the valley and over the hill to a promise of what is to come.

Prayer

Blessed Lord, we cry out to you, in this hour of need, doubt, and concern. Though we believe and have committed our lives to you, we feel faint of heart and slow of action. While we desire to live in faith, challenges arise that are major obstacles to living out faith. Praying feels like uttering empty words. Worship seems uninspired. In this wilderness of disjointed reality, make us whole and shore up our faith. Let our faith be that of the mustard seed, that it may grow into a tree of strong belief. Anoint our eyes, ears, and heart that we may be moved as we prepare to worship and witness to others about all you have done for us. We so adore you, Loving God, that we are embarrassed to think or speak words of doubt. Yet, even in the most difficult times, we know that you care, that you have heard our prayers and our cries. For this we give thanks. Bless our faith community that our lives may become a beacon to all, signaling that you are real, that you love us, and that you can and will heal all of our doubts and fears.

Litany

Leader: Despite our best intentions, our prayers, our best plan-
            ning, our well-disciplined spiritual lives, we confess
            that we experience doubt and disbelief.

People: **When our faith runs thin and our doubts over-
            whelm us, we give thanks that God cares and loves
            us still; we have but to look to the hills from which
            our help does come.**

Leader: Like the psalmist, we know moments of doubt. Like
            Jesus at Golgotha, we cry out, "My God, My God, why
            have you forsaken me?" Why have you forsaken us?

People: **Even in days when we feel abandoned and all alone,
            we rejoice that like the psalmist, we know that God
            made the world, God made us, and God truly cares.**

Leader: We rejoice that scripture tells us of God's great prom-
            ises and covenants with us, of God's undying commit-
            ment to us.

People: **From day to day, whatever comes our way, we cele-
            brate our God-given faith, which fuels all of our
            relationships. We are not ashamed of our doubt, but
            we accept it with faith.**

Benediction

Having been renewed and restored, having shared our doubts
and concerns, we go forth to be beacons of light and hope,
reflecting God's radiance to all of God's children! God be with
you always; go now in peace. Amen.

19. Fear

There is no fear in love, but perfect love casts out fear. For fear has to do
with punishment, and he who fears is not perfected in love.
—1 John 4:18

Quotation

Wasn't that what happened to Lot's wife? A loyalty to old things, a fear of the new, a fear to change, to look ahead?" (Toni Cade Bambara, writer, editor)

Invocation

Our strong God, our ever-present God, as we enter into this temple to worship and offer praise, help us bring our fears to the altar and present them to you, that we might be fully present to glorify your name! Let us worship God!

Reflections

There are times when we shut down, either because we are so overwhelmed, or because we have experienced trauma and the only way we can cope with such fear is to shut down completely. No matter the strength of our support systems, our intellect, or our financial worth, fear is a normal human emotion. All fear is not bad. Fear can protect us from hurtful experiences, like walking in front of a moving truck; fear can make sure that we are careful. If fear becomes overwhelming to the point that we are paralyzed, we need to get help and support. We can seek counseling and spiritual direction, and we can keep a journal. Extreme fear may require intense therapy. Just as we encourage people to seek help for physical matters, we must also encourage them to get assistance when they experience emotional difficulty. Sometimes boys and men have difficulty expressing their fear and other emotions because when they were infants, barely walking, they were made to stop crying; they were told, "You are a man!" What kind of cruelty do we daily perpetrate when we insist that a male child is a man, that he cannot cry because that makes him a wimp? Where does his rage go? Where does the rage or fear of our girls go when we do not allow them appropriate ways to express their anger or feelings of dread? A faithful life allows us to express our deepest feelings in healthy ways. A faithful life also allows us to experience a positive fear in relation to God—a profound reverence and awe.

Prayer

Blessed God, from everlasting to everlasting, even when we know fear, you are and have been God and our dwelling place, for which we offer thanksgiving. In you, we have sanctuary, a place of refuge and safety. When we know fear, we may also be uncertain about what we believe and how to make decisions. There are days when we are so troubled, that we hesitate and do not know which way to turn. We bless you, for because of your grace, we can be who we are without pretense. Divine Creator, you have room for our fear and uncertainty. In you, we experience inspiration, which gives us permission to excel and grow or to know fear and doubt. Sometimes we get confused about our priorities and shift to the realm of idolatry. Sometimes the trials and tribulations of life press us toward distrust and a lack of confidence. In the process of life, we sometimes ask questions when we do not understand, when we hurt and are in pain. So great is your love and mercy that, even when we know fear, your guidance and advocacy help us come to a resolution. We will come to embrace the persons, places, or things that can be supportive of our development. When we monitor ourselves and are good stewards of all of our resources, doubt can be a catalyst for renewed faith.

Litany

Leader: When we think about life, there is much we cannot know, which sometimes causes us fear. Because we trust in God, fear need not control us. In not knowing, we walk by faith.

People: **Fear relies on a false sense of reality, on what appears to be so. We imagine that something is real, but in reality it only seems so. As our thoughts about what may happen are usually worse than what really will happen, we ask for guidance and clarity, O God.**

Leader: Fear is an emotion that has the value of protecting us from dangerous situations. For this kind of human radar, we give thanks, and we pledge to be good stewards of this gift.

People: **The same fear that protects us may also keep us from fully experiencing the marvelous opportunities God makes available for us.**

Leader: In facing every awakening reality, fear is the gift of being fully present and aware of the many blessings of God that come our way moment by moment.

People: **We rejoice and give a thousand prayers of thanksgiving that we are not overcome by fear, for we walk by faith with God eternal.**

Benediction

As we embark on a moment-by-moment, healthy, inspired life with God, we go now to rejoice and spread the gospel of love and peace! God be with you always; go now in peace. Amen.

—ɯ—

20. Grief

*My eyes are spent with weeping; /my soul is in tumult; /my heart is poured
out in grief /because of the destruction of the daughter of my people,
/because infants and babes faint /in the streets of the city.*
—Lamentations 2:11

Quotation

Death is a part of life and . . . grieving is a natural reaction
to the loss of a loved one. . . . Grief comes in many guises
and . . . no one kind of loss is more or less worthy of grief
than any other." (Arlene H. Churn, Baptist minister and certi-
fied Grief Counsel Specialist, and Janet Hill)

Invocation

God of Life and Death, Author of Creation, bring our hearts,
minds, and spirits into this present moment, that we might be
fully present to worship you as we honor the experience of
grief as a part of the continuum of your grace. Let us worship
God!

Reflections

With all of our technological advances, with the written annals
of history, and with the knowledge that death is a part of life, we
still do not handle death well. Whether death is a culmination
of a long illness or an accident—death shocks most of us.
Because we tend to deny death, we often fail to take advantage
of the rituals and coping mechanisms available to us in order to
shift from denial to deep loss in a healthy manner. Many factors
influence whether or not we allow ourselves to experience grief.
Grief is an experience of deep and poignant distress. Deep disappointment, bereavement, mourning, or loss may trigger grief or
deep sorrow. Because we are convinced that everything needs to

be accomplished quickly, we do not allow ourselves time to grieve and mourn. We expect people to "just get over it." Grief is a process that takes as long as it takes. To extend a time for mourning is a blessing. When persons have been critically important to our lives, there is a void when they die. Thus, we may experience desolation and depression; we may be cranky, short tempered, or discombobulated. In the hustle and bustle of our dizzying schedules, we unconsciously avoid having time on our hands to stand naked before God's presence, to feel the pain of loss and the depths of our grief. To take time to grieve is to honor the life and commitment of our beloved friend or family member. To grieve is to honor God for the gift of that relationship, and slowly to begin the process of healing. We will never forget these persons, for when they are gone their spirits are forever in our hearts.

Prayer

Blessed Comforter, all the songs and anointings with oil failed to stay the voice of death, the deluge of pain; this deep void is in our lives. We come to you at this hour, for we know within your presence and in our church community, there are tons of hope and acres of faith to shoulder our coliseums of pain. Embrace us with love, cloak us with faith; let your mercy sustain our spirituality. As the storms of life continue to rage, when stress, suffering, confusion, and pandemonium wrench us from the safety of certainty, we feel your presence and benevolence, your care and compassion. In good times and bad, between human frailty and ferocity, in all of our needs, doubts, fears, greed, and misgivings—you are our companion. You bless us with others who bring comfort, confidence, courage, and charity. When the agony presses us to destruction, we rejoice to hear your voice saying, "Peace, be still!" "I am with you always." We bless you for loving us so, for walking with us as we grieve our loss. Weeping does come for many days and nights, but joy does come in the morning.

Litany

Leader: Rejoice! Hallelujah! All praises to God for the gift of life, eternal life, and the moment of death, which opens the door to life everlasting.

People: **Blessed are you, great God; you are with us every moment of life and are present with us at our death. Bless us that we might live each moment, cherishing the time we have alone and with others as privilege.**

Leader: From generation to generation let us remember our ancestors, our stories. Help these difficult times be times of celebration and remembrance; let us so honor each other as we live, that there are no regrets when we come to die.

People: **Blessed are you merciful God; you bless us with seasons, times to live and times to die. Help us have peace knowing that as we are born to live, the time will come when we are to die.**

Leader: Help us die easy when the time comes. Bless all who give care to the dying. We pray that we can be a comforting presence when friends and family are in transition from this life to the next.

People: **Blessings and honor, courage and hope to all who have come to the end of their lives and those who walk with them during this time of their journey. May we know the joyous experience of resurrected love and peace.**

Benediction

As the sun rises and sets, as we are born, live, and die, may our love of God and of life ever sustain us as we go out to be with the

living and stand in witness to the dying. God be with you always;
go now in peace. Amen.

—ɯ—

21. Life

Only let your manner of life be worthy of the gospel of Christ,
so that whether I come and see you or am absent, I may
hear of you that you stand firm in one spirit, with one
mind striving side by side for the faith of the gospel.
—Philippians 1:27

Quotation

When you're looking at yourself in the mirror you have
to remember that that image is only a part of you. The
you inside. If you have any kind of brain at all, and
kind of sense of self, you realize how unique that is. Nobody can
be you. Uniqueness needs to be celebrated. There's only one of
you. You're totally and absolutely individual. . . . Self-definition
is very important. You define who you are by actions, by what
you do with your life." (Judith Jamison, dancer, choreographer,
artistic director, Alvin Ailey's American Dance Theatre)

Invocation

The hour has come to worship God, giving thanks for life, opening our hearts, minds, and spirits for this time of celebration. Let
us worship God!

Reflections

When we continue to compartmentalize our lives, we diminish
our capacity to learn, grow, be healthy, and have a fully

dynamic relationship with God. As human beings, we are so complex and integrally connected that any time something goes askew in one part of our system, the other part cannot help but be affected. Getting in tune with one's sacredness requires attentiveness to health, faith, and spirituality. Life as gift involves the workings of God in the splendor of nature. Life is wonderfully beautiful; life can also be full of confusion, rage, and pain. In those moments, we pray, realizing that we can never underestimate living in present time. The gift of *present time* is the gift of living in the moment, in the newness, in gratitude for life itself, even with its foibles. Such a life of gratitude and thanksgiving becomes the hallmark of a balanced life, a life in which we can take responsibility and not always be quick to project our insecurities, illnesses, and inefficiencies on others, making them our scapegoats. In thanksgiving, we experience God's holiness in a more profound way, just as we come to see our own sacredness and begin to create life as sanctuary for ourselves and others.

Prayer

Precious God, there are moments when we become so filled with the details that we forget the big picture of why we are here on the earth. We forget the covenant invitation to love ourselves, love our neighbors, and love life. We often forget the source of life and the many special moments we share over a lifetime. Be with us now, that we might reconnect with you and gain a sense of the power and meaning of life itself. Bless us to know that we have value, that we can make a difference. As we worship today, let us feel you, the very fiber and essence of life. We give thanks that you so value our lives that you protect us, even when we sometimes embark on dangerous paths. We thank you for the many rewarding experiences that come our way. In the moments when we begin to take life for granted, please gently remind us of how precious and blessed this life is. Help us have empathy. Give us the ability to walk in the shoes of our sisters and our brothers, transcending judgment, moving toward healthy compassion. Please give us discernment that we might know when to speak, when to be silent, when to help another by taking action, and when to help as silent witness. Help us see and correct dysfunctional lifestyles and behaviors, so that our lives reflect a legacy of you.

Litany

Leader: We love to tell the story of life: of God, our Creator; of Jesus the Christ, the incarnation of love; and of the Holy Spirit, our Advocate, the One who empowers us spiritually.

People: **As spiritual beings, we come to share our stories of God's love and salvation. We know the pain and the plenty that accompany our faithful lives, and we desire to have the courage to be true to our call.**

Leader: We love to tell stories of God working throughout history, stories that speak of God's wonderful love for creation, of God's care, God's mercy, and God's steadfastness—eternal in scope, brilliant in origins, complex in diversity and versatility.

People: **As spiritual beings, we know the power of the unexplainable in life, the majesty of faithful reconciliation of the irreconcilable, the splendidness of grace in doing the undoable.**

Leader: We know the joy of song, prayer, and dance as we praise God with our voices, our thoughts, our bodies, many becoming one in that great communion of the church universal—that global, magnificent, growing, loving community of faith.

People: As faithful beings, we accept God's call on our lives and we make a joyful noise for the gift of salvation and the freedom that comes with such grace.

Benediction

As we leave this temple of worship, may we all go in peace and anticipation, celebrating the life we have been given, honoring the lives of those who made it possible for us to be, and daily honoring God, the Giver and Guarantor of life. God be with you always; go now in peace. Amen.

22. Accomplishment/ Achievement

[Jesus said], "I glorified You on the earth, having accomplished the work which You have given Me to do."
—John 17:4 (NASB)

Quotation

As long as you keep a person down, some part of you has to be down there to hold [him/her] down, so it means you cannot soar as you otherwise might." (Marian Anderson [1897–1993], international singer, United Nations Delegate, Recipient of the Presidential Medal of Freedom and the Congressional Medal of Honor)

Invocation

To the One who labors with us and allows us to make accomplishments and achieve greatness in life: Blessed art thou! To you be all honor and glory; your achievements are more numerous than the molecules in the air! How awesome are your works. How blessed to be in your presence as you gather us that we might adore you for all creation.

Reflections

Marian Anderson, who had her humble beginnings in Philadelphia, Pennsylvania, is one of the twentieth century's most distinguished opera singers. What must it have been like for her to sing at the Lincoln Memorial, Easter Sunday, 1939, at the invitation of Eleanor

Roosevelt! The Daughters of the American Revolution, owners of Washington's Constitution Hall, had disrespected Anderson and not allowed her to sing on their "sacred" stage. In God's infinite design, working through Eleanor Roosevelt, Anderson sang that Easter, before the Lincoln Memorial, to an audience of 75,000. In 1991, she received a Grammy Award for her lifetime achievement. We may say that such a story only happens once in a lifetime, but we have no idea what God may call us to do, and what influence one achievement can have. Many heroes, male and female, have humble beginnings. Some have the luxury of every possible educational and cultural opportunity. Others do not. What the great artists, scholars, and leaders have in common is a passion for what they do, and they work hard. God's grace allows many of us to do ordinary, and rather amazing, things: walk, talk, breathe, learn many languages, do complex medical procedures, perform unbelievable athletic feats, become leaders of universities, state governments, and corporations, and build nonprofit entities to aid those in need. All of these achievements and accomplishments are opportunities made possible by God. We each have talents: Are we courageous enough to use these talents and help others in the process?

Prayer

Blessed *El Shaddai*, God all sufficient, your mighty gifts and graces to us are so amazing that they could only come from your generous covenantal love. We appreciate the tremendous growth and development we see in the world. You have blessed us so that, as people on earth, we have seen so many changes in our lifetime: instead of walking and riding horses we are driving cars and flying planes; a farming society has become one of incredible technological advances. So often, God, we are running too fast, trying to do so much that we end up going in circles. As you continue to help us achieve, help us enjoy each step in the development of the process, not just the finished product. Help us savor the early rough ideas, the dreams, and the visions. Help us carefully select the time, the place, and the persons we will collaborate with to achieve our goals. Bless us so that we might always discern an ethical manner in which to advance our ideas. Let us not trouble over results; let us not envy those who may get there before we do. Open our hearts and spirits that we might only participate in those activities that glorify you. Please be with our children. As we fumble in parenting, sometimes we hinder our children's creativity out of ignorance and fear. Bless us to know that each child is special. Each child has something to achieve, and he or she can achieve it when loved unconditionally.

Litany

Leader:　To work with our hands and minds, and hearts and spirits, is an opportunity to celebrate the gifts God has given us. In using these gifts, we can create, collaborate, share, and give.

People:　**Blessed be the One who equips us to enjoy the thrill of accomplishment, the joy of sharing others' achievements, and the holiness of peace.**

Leader:　As we think and write, cook and clean, design and create, plant and sow—as we do all things large and small, we celebrate infinite daily moments in tune with God.

People:　**As far as the east is from the west, so is the vastness of your loving Spirit and your loving artistry in the universe. We are humbled that you afford us the gifts of learning, remembering, and story telling.**

Leader:　Let us tell our stories, share our accomplishments, and release envy as destructive energy that inhibits our ability to be full of joy and to experience completion.

People:　**In our lives, we pledge to recognize all accomplishments, in order to acknowledge and encourage**

God's rule in our lives and to build healthy communities that achieve in solidarity.

Benediction

In the morning, noon, and evening of our lives, may we each stand on God's promises and embrace our God-given gifts. May we share, inspire, and love. May we learn from mistakes, rejoice for the lessons, and daily offer thanks to the Author, Sustainer, and Finisher of our faith. God be with you always; go now in peace. Amen.

—∿∿—

23. Education

And the Lord's servant must not be quarrelsome but kindly to every one,
an apt teacher, forbearing.
—2 Timothy 2:24

Quotation

Both class and race survived education, and neither should. What is education then? If it doesn't help a human being to recognize that humanity is humanity, what is it for? So you can make a bigger salary than other people?" (Beah Richards [1920–2000] actor, playwright, poet)

Invocation

Great Teacher of teachers, we enter into this sanctuary blessed with the ability to read, write, and think. Help us come together in one accord, ever open for the Holy Spirit to teach and guide us as we come now to worship God!

Reflections

Education in the healthiest sense is a dynamic, amazing process of love, discernment, cooperation, anticipation, hope, and growth. The practice of education is one of developing persons mentally, morally, or aesthetically, especially by instruction and facilitation. Education involves the training of ourselves and others by informal and formal means, including instruction and supervised practice of knowledge, skills, trades, or professions. Education is a process of sharing information. None of us needs to know everything in the world to make it, but it ameliorates if we can write and read. Often trouble emerges because someone misreads, or does not read something carefully. Many get into difficulty because of poor communication. When we read, write, and learn to communicate successfully, we realize that we are not alone. We learn that many of the things we think are unique are not unique after all. Many wonderful venues open to us when we experience education. We can bless our faith lives by reading sacred texts and works of inspiration. By thinking critically and getting clearer about what we believe, we are better able to share and be good stewards of our resources. When education is blessing, we leave the quagmire of greed and desperation and move to places of generosity and abundance.

Prayer

Mother/Father of us all, help us make sense out of our confused minds. Building on your love and gifts of faith, help us teach and learn; help us educate ourselves and others in dignity, honor, and joy. Bless our faith, that we might seek your guidance before developing curricula and study materials. Help us clarify the priorities in our lives. As we work more and more hours, we seem to have less and less—less time, fewer financial resources, fewer inspiring moments, and less time to dream dreams. Give us wisdom so that we may be good stewards of all our resources, especially the resources of education, time, and finances. Help us know the gift and the beauty of the human mind, body, and spirit. Give us a desire to educate the whole person in all walks of life, for all generations. Blessed God, we trust you for religious and spiritual issues but not for all aspects of our lives. Help us to be open to your grace and creativity in everything, including our thinking. Send your clouds by day and your pillars of fire by night to be our guides. May the educational programs we create be faithful and morally sound; may they offer healthy stimulation for our minds and our hearts, ever resting on your divinely given wisdom.

Litany

Leader: How magnificent are the gifts of knowledge that we share—gifts of reading, writing, thinking, learning, and decision-making. We honor your teaching, O God, the architect of all knowledge, the anointer of all teachers.

People: **Hallelujah for these gifts of knowledge. May we always hold these gifts and the opportunity to learn in trust, for many will never see the inside of a schoolhouse.**

Leader: How miraculous are the gifts of poets and artists, the calculations of mathematicians and scientists, the ingenuities of engineers and athletes as they perform, create, design, and invent incredible feats of artistry, expressions of God.

People: **Blessed is the Giver of all creative and learned gifts. May we support all people as they work to express their God-given talent without envy.**

Leader: For our first teachers, those who patiently guide our fertile minds to reach beyond, to explore the vast mysterious world, those who encourage us in our squiggly writing and our stumbling over multiplication tables—for their soft voices and their forgetfulness, we give thanks.

People: **For all the ways in which education and knowledge help to heal nations, grow communities, and strengthen understanding, Hallelujah! Forgive our misuse of education and knowledge; forgive us when we slight the knowledge and education of others. For these gifts, we give thanks.**

Benediction

As we plan to leave this temple of worship, help us be teachers and learners, educators and pupils on the highways and byways of life, ever serving you and giving witness to your people, spreading the good news of the gospel—the gospel of peace. God be with you always; go now in peace. Amen.

24. Entrepreneurship

One who heard us was a woman named Lydia, from the city of Thyatira, a seller of purple goods, who was a worshiper of God. The Lord opened her heart to give heed to what was said by Paul.
—Acts 16:14

Quotation

My generation sees little separation between the traditional spiritual function of the church and the need for black political and economic parity [entrepreneurship].

We are demanding that the black church . . . regardless of denomination . . . respond, or African Americans risk reenslavement on all fronts. . . . Today's ministry must preach that Money is God in action." (Beverly Hall Lawrence, journalist)

Invocation

Welcome to God's temple, where we gather to honor God for the many blessings of life and for the gifts of entrepreneurship and creativity! Let us worship God!

Reflections

When we think back on the beginnings of peoples of African descent in this country, not only do we recall the deep oppression, insanity, and cruelty of slavery, but also the economics, the money matters that required and ultimately sanctioned this heinous experience. Slave owners were entrepreneurs. They had their own businesses and worked to plant and harvest their crops, using human beings of African descent as chattel, as brood mares and stud bulls. Some people would rather forget this awful part of our past. But forgetting will not change reality. Forgetting does not prepare us to live in the twenty-first century and deal with on-going oppression or our opportunities to now be in charge, to have businesses, to be entrepreneurs. Some of us are afraid to have our own businesses. Others have attempted to do so, but failed because of poor planning and insufficient capital. The gift of having a business or of collaborating with others in business is having greater say about the final product or service. We also have more opportunities to help our community and employ persons who might otherwise not have a chance. Can we get over our intraracial racism, sexism, classism, and homophobia so that we can work together and avoid tearing each other down over pettiness, while all other immigrants keep advancing?

Prayer

Precious, eternal God, thank you for the many complex gifts of creativity. When we do see the depths of blessing given us, we are overwhelmed to tears. These tears of joy proclaim that we cannot understand your loving generosity. Your gifts have inspired many to do great things: to dream, invent, carve, dance, write, explore, and ponder. These are the gifts of entrepreneurship. Give us wisdom to embrace the tools of business for our personal improvement, and for the improvement of those in our community, especially our church community. God, some of us are trapped and burdened by tradition. We are so wedded to what Mama and Papa did that we often fail to see that if Mama and Papa were here today, they would be embracing the new ways and new ideas instead of being stuck in the past. Help us honor traditions and our ancestors, but do not let that reference become a stumbling block for new congregational economic development. Bless us to envision how we can invest and grow businesses as ministry. When failures come, help us resist discouragement. Help us make trustworthy alliances that can support our business ventures. Let us always remember to give you the glory and to avoid making an idol of any gift given by you.

Litany

Leader: God give us the ways and means to live, grow, and work, to support our families and communities as entrepreneurs.

People: **We rejoice in gratitude for the creative ways that God has led us to invest and grow businesses in our communities, and we rejoice for those entrepreneurs who share their gifts with us.**

Leader: As a church body, we know that our commission is one of ministry. Bless us to see that ministries of economic growth are opportunities for us to do your work on earth.

People: **We acknowledge our fear and trepidation in moving toward new ventures. When our pettiness dampens the spirit of entrepreneurs who want to go forward and help us grow, please help us be more open to change.**

Leader: We confess our envy and jealousy of others who do progressive things for the church. We also confess our desire to embrace new ministries and know that entrepreneurship can be one vehicle of change.

People: **As a community wounded by oppression, keep us from self-destructing, and bless us to not be tricked into fraud or bad investments as we embrace entre-preneurship as a ministry that can further spread the gospel.**

Benediction

We go from here, not from the temple of moneychangers, but as a temple of grace and growth, committed to using entrepreneurship as a tool for Christian witness. God be with you always; go now in peace. Amen.

25. Dignity

"Deck yourself with majesty and dignity; clothe yourself
with glory and splendor."
—Job 40:10

Quotation

When the [African American] learns what manner of [person] s/he is spiritually, s/he will wake up all over. S/he will stop playing white even on the stage. S/he will rise in the majesty of his/her own soul. S/he will glorify the beauty of his/her own brown skin. S/he will stop thinking white and go to thinking straight and living right. S/he will realize that wrong-reaching, wrong-bleaching, and wrong-mixing have 'most nigh ruin't them and s/he will redeem [their] body and rescue [their] soul from the bondage of that death." (Nannie Helen Burroughs [1883–1961] organizer, educator, journalist)

Invocation

Noble, wise, and ever-living God, bring us into this worship with our minds fixed on you, as we honor your dignity, the dignity for which you have anointed us. We invite a new Pentecost in our hearts as we embrace you in all respect and appreciation.

Reflections

The quiet dignity emitted by those blessed to live past their 70s, 80s, and 90s, is the same elegance and tentativeness that registers with little ones when they take their first steps. If we are wise, we will realize how truly blessed we are to be in the company of such angels. Jesus tells us to be attentive to how we greet others, for we may be in the company of angels. The good news must be evoked and shared with dignity, respect, and consideration for those whom we wish to empower. In sharing from a place of dignity, we impart dignity to those we minister to, and in turn, they help us grow. Some will not want to hear the good news. Others might be suspicious. Grounded in grace and dignity, we embody a certainty that invites others to listen. When we come from desperation, pushiness, and judgment, others will not want to listen. We, ourselves, do not wish to listen when people speak to us in curt, harsh, or fearful tones. To honor our own dignity and the dignity of others is to nurture self-respect and self-esteem. A graced life is one of healthy pride, not self-centeredness; of sharing and assurance, not greed and uneasiness. Shared dignity is a testament to the grace, dignity, and elegance of God.

Prayer

Beloved God of the universe, the Creator and sustainer of all dignity and value for human life, we thank you for the gifts of dignity and blessed pride that allow us to honor you in all that we do with elegance and poise. We honor this sense of dignity by not making others feel inferior or indicating that we think we are superior. We honor your dignity and your gift of dignity to us as a sign and symbol of the covenant you have made. As we honor your blessed dignity, instill in our spirits a sense of discernment, that we not make idols or gods of anything or anyone, including ourselves. We see your dignity in the vastness and wonders of the universe. Great and glorious is all of your creation. Great and glorious is the gift of dignity. Through the anointing of the Holy Spirit, may we live consecrated lives of peace and tranquillity. May we build communities where everyone's dignity and personhood is respected. May we teach and guide others with a commitment to excellence, relying on the light of your presence. We open up our hearts and we lift our eyes to you, as we hold fast to your love, dignity, and redeeming Spirit.

Litany

Leader: We magnify the love and dignity of God, seeing the light of God within each of us—in worship, at home, at play—providing a witness to God's remarkable, awe-inspiring countenance.

People: **Glory, glory, glory to you God. Heaven and earth are full of your magnificent dignity. We pause and we pray as your power washes over us and cleanses us of our doubts and fears.**

Leader: In love and joy, we fear you; we respect who you are, and all that you have done for us. We claim our own dignity as a witness to your special grandeur.

People: **Help us to see with our eyes and hear with our ears the wonderful testimonies of your graced dignity throughout nature, and in our families and our communities.**

Leader: The peace and grace of Christ represents the quiet dignity of God. We honor that blessedness, and we pray and work without ceasing to share these special blessings wherever we are called to serve and love.

People: **Blessed quietness, holy joy! We give reverence to the blessed dignity of God. We honor this grace in each moment as we encounter new life, new hope, new joy in God and community.**

Benediction

Blessed Lord, as we leave this place consecrated for worshiping you, please guide and order our steps, that we might teach and embody the nobility of Spirit given in love. Give us the courage to daily respect ourselves and others, celebrating your gift of dignity to us. God be with you always; go now in peace. Amen.

—⟋⟍⟋—

26. Music

It is good to give thanks to the LORD, */to sing praises to thy name, O Most High; /to declare thy steadfast love in the morning, /and thy faithfulness by night, /to the music of the lute and the harp, /to the melody of the lyre.*
—Psalm 92:1-3

Quotation

I believe very strongly that the way Africans and African music is practiced, composed, and performed embodies a set of values that ought to be applied in the broader society. Part of that is allowing yourself to be open, not controlling. Cooperation as opposed to competition." (Ysaye Barnwell, American ASL interpreter, speech pathologist, community activist, singer, member of *Sweet Honey in the Rock)*

Invocation

Oh rejoice with glad tidings and great joy, for now is the hour of celebration, of lifting our voices in music and words, as we invoke all that is holy. Let us worship God!

Reflections

For some, the notion of having a love affair with God is appalling and blasphemous, and perhaps this is to be expected. But when we think about the awesomeness and the power of anointing that exists at the singing of Handel's *Messiah*, Dorsey's "Precious Lord, Take My Hand," Smallwood's "Total Praise," Bond's arrangement of "He's Got the Whole World in His Hands," or Campbell's "He'll Understand and Say Well Done," how can we not experience a love affair with God? The great Duke Ellington once proclaimed, "Music is my mistress." Music brings us to a close, intimate, transcendental experience of God. Countless sermons and testimonies exist on the importance of having a relationship with God. Close relationships are intimate. If we are really moved by God and desire God, then we are intrigued by God. Paul speaks of the scandal of the gospel. The notions of relationship, intimacy, intrigue, and scandal are synonyms for the term *affair*. Music allows a daily affair with God. Music engenders awesome experiences and moves us in a profound manner; the stories and sleaze in many tabloid papers pale in comparison. Tabloid stories sensationalize. Music sung for God thrills and transforms. Having a daily affair with God through music refashions our day and helps us embrace an affair of a lifetime—an affair with God.

Prayer

Blessed God, you give the gifts of music that allow us to praise, to bring joy and pleasure, to inspire. We honor the offerings of the ministry of music. We bless you and all of those who have given tirelessly in creating, composing, and performing music. Just as angelic choruses were heard singing at the birth of Jesus, we hear the voices of angels, anointed by you, in our worship services, on recordings, and on the radio. We give thanks for the gifts of music that we create as families and friends, that we can enjoy alone and with company. Whereas languages and particular cultural practices come with boundaries, music is often the universal gift. We can share together for you have given us these talents. We are so blessed to know that the most important priority in life will not be our accomplishments, our stock portfolio, the children's activities, the latest gossip, making ends meet, having an exciting social calendar, or advancing our careers. The sharing of music, and fully experiencing its profound effect upon each of us, shows us that only you are worthy of praise. May each note be that "Balm in Gilead" that can make the wounded whole.

Litany

Leader: O make a joyful noise unto God, all people, with instruments and voices and dance and singing. For music is a gift from God to be used in praise and adoration, and to inspire others.

People: **We lift our hearts and voices in song. We come elated and inspired, moved and persuaded to join with others in singing hymns, gospels, anthems, and praise songs.**

Leader: We give thanks for those musicians called by God to lead and guide and inspire through making music. May they experience renewal and joy as we lift you up in song.

People: **All of God's people rejoice in song, in the music of organ, piano, trumpet, drums, flutes, and horns, and in liturgical dance! Rejoice, rejoice, rejoice, O people of God, of Jerusalem, of Zion.**

Leader: O sing and play instruments, hum and sing obbligato, for great is the gift of music that lets everything in our being and our realities praise God.

People: **We shout, Hosanna! Hallelujah! Hallelujah! For great is God's faithfulness and love; great is our love for God. How blessed are we to make music in God's honor!**

Benediction

We rejoice with uplifted hearts and inspired spirits, and now as we depart, let us go and spread the loving, graced-filled messages of music and song to those who await the good news! God be with you always; go now in peace. Amen.

—⁓—

27. Responsibility

Then they said to [Jonah], "Tell us on whose account this evil has come upon us. What is your occupation? And whence do you come? What is your country? And of what people are you?"
—Jonah 1:8

Quotation

I leave you love . . . hope . . . the challenge of developing confidence in one another . . . a thirst for education . . . a respect for the uses of power . . . faith . . . racial dignity . . . a desire to live harmoniously with your fellow [human beings] . . . a responsibility to our young people." (Mary McCleod Bethune [1875–1955], educator; political leader; founder and first president of the National Council of Negro Women; founder of Bethune Cookman College, Daytona Beach, Florida)

Invocation

Majestic, loving God, we greet you and bless your presence as you invite us to be responsible stewards of all our resources, as we give ourselves to total praise for your grace, your mercy, and the covenantal relationships we share. Let us worship in love.

Reflections

We often think of responsibility as a burden, something that is difficult and taxing; though not inherently complex and challenging, it may be and often is. Responsibility is an opportunity to be in charge, accountable, answerable for something or someone; it requires us to be trustworthy and able to make the best choices. Being responsible means taking care of getting the job done and done well. Thus, when we give our word, we will make the plans and the contacts, do the work, and have a full report. Being responsible may simply refer to showing up on time and being prepared. Responsibility is one key component of stewardship, the judicious and respectful use of our resources. Thus being responsible within one's family means supporting the ebb and flow of work and sharing at home. To be responsible on one's job means to be punctual, to do the expected work, to have a pleasant demeanor, and to support the mission of the particular agency, firm, or organization. To be responsible in one's faith community means to participate by showing up for worship, by contributing one's talents in the appropriate ministries, by praying for individuals and the larger community, by contributing financially, and by studying scripture and other books that encourage growth in grace. When one experiences responsibility as commitment, there can be joy.

Prayer

Living, faithful God, as creatures on the wonderful planet Earth, we give thanks that your love sustains us and our environment. When we think of all you do for us and all of the responsibility you take on our behalf, we are humbled and amazed. As we move into each day, we pray for the courage and grace to see that day as an opportunity to be responsible stewards in every area of our life. Help us to use all of our moral, social, and financial capital in intelligent, sensible, and balanced ways. We desire to make choices out of appreciation for the gifts that we have, not out of fear or trembling. Help us be aware of our global citizenry, that we may speak to all people with dignity and respect, that we may avoid stereotypes, that we not make any group of people scape-goats simply because we feel bad and need to blame someone when we hurt. We ask for a release from envy and greed. May we learn to plan ahead, take advantage of our opportunities, and live a balanced life. We have been entrusted with the responsi-bility for gifts and resources made possible by God, and we desire to be worthy of this responsibility and this level of trust. May we come to appreciate fully God's gifts held by us in trust.

Litany

Leader: In the beginning, God created the world. God created us and gave humanity responsibility for the use of the earth. May we live in covenant accountability.

People: **As committed believers, as stewards, we hold the gifts of God to us in trust, ever mindful of the Source of our gifts, and the need for us to use them with care.**

Leader: Daily, we are called to honor our lives, our vocations, and our relationships as sacred and holy.

People: **Blessed are those who embody the commitments of stewardship, ever balancing how we use our resources with the particular call God has on our lives.**

Leader: Glory to God in the highest, in heaven and on earth, and peace to all God's people; may the day come when no one hungers for food or for righteousness, for the earth belongs to God.

People: **We celebrate our responsibility to God to be in rela-tionship, to take care of the environment, and to use the resources that we need, never taking that which we do not need.**

Benediction

In the beauty of the day, in the beauty of your hearts, may you embrace the responsibilities that are of God; may you accept the call God has on your life from this day forward as you live responsibly, in health, in stability, in peace. God be with you always; go now in peace. Amen.

—⟋ɯ⟍—

28. Sexuality

Come, my beloved—let us go out early to the vineyards, and see whether the vines have budded, whether the grape blossoms have opened and the pomegranates are in bloom. There I will give you my love.
—Song of Solomon 7:11-12

Quotation

The reality of Black bodies as icons points the way to the fact that this is a sexually repressive culture although the media, the church, and even our personal observations may indicate that we are promiscuous. We are sexually repressed in the sense that we have made all kinds of compromises regarding our sexuality to live on this planet and in our society and to survive in the church. . . . We are sexually repressed while at the same time being sexually active, and this is a dangerous combination. We don't understand how our bodies function or how the bodies of our sexual partners function. We fumble in the dark regarding subjects like teenage pregnancy. Time and again children repeat the all too familiar litany, 'I never thought it would happen to me'; and when asked if they were using any form of birth control the answer is a resounding no. That is a manifestation of sexual repression." (Emilie Townes, scholar, author, ordained minister, Christian social ethicist)

Invocation

Creator God, you made our bodies, our sexuality, our capacity to love. As we embark on this worship experience, help us honor you and be comfortable in our own bodies, as graced sexual beings, who come to celebrate you and this powerful gift of passion and love.

Reflections

Whenever you want to get a snicker or hear people laugh nervously or get people to blush and hover around embarrassed, mention the word sex. People become nervous talking about sex, and create euphemisms or substitute words, rather than use the biological terms like vagina, penis, clitoris, hymen, scrotum, breasts, or testicles. We make sure our two- and three-year-olds can clearly enunciate re-fri-ger-a-tor, but would rather have them learn nonsensical names when it comes to male and female genitalia. That which has been created beautiful and that which gives tremendous pleasure has been stereotyped as nasty, forbidden, or ugly. Simply put, sex concerns the pleasurable total of the genital structural, functional, and behavioral characteristics of living beings; sex directly promotes the welfare and well-being of interacting persons, which, incidentally and integrally, usually places them in categories of the male and female genders. Some children of God identify themselves as intrasexual, transgendered, bisexual, or homosexual. Scientists, even endocrinologists, know so little about what it means to be a sexual being, particularly as it relates to delineating sexual identity. Sexuality is the quality or state of being sexual, an involvement with sex. Sex is beautiful, orgasmic, phenomenal. The highest state of sexual intercourse is communion, Eucharist, where two souls, two spirits experience the full impact of their Creator's grace. The Creator imbued humans with sexuality when creating humans in the *Imago Dei*.

Sexual activity should not, and is not intended to, be entered into casually or thoughtlessly. Engaging in sexual activity calls for maturity, commitment, wisdom, insight, and grace into the profundity of the gift of sexuality between consenting adults.

Prayer

Beloved Creator, masterful engineer who designs our bodies and gives us the gift of sexuality: Help us know that we are made sacred and that our bodies are temples of your Holy Spirit, made to be loved and honored, not desecrated by improper and unfeeling sexual activity. When we desire to exploit and be careless with the gift of sexuality, send angels to quiet our hearts and our libido, to quiet our sexual urges, so that we might not dishonor our bodies, our spirits, or you, by entering into regrettable behavior. Help parents and guardians have wisdom in teaching children about sex and sexuality. Help us to become comfortable with fully experiencing our sexuality when it is appropriate—as mature, consenting, knowledgeable adults who are in covenant with our partner. Help our churches prepare curricula that will teach grace-filled abstinence in a way that is not fear-based nor guilt-ridden. Help us to love our bodies and to be comfortable as sexual beings. We pray for sex predators and sex offenders. Grant us the wisdom to never hold the victim responsible for being raped, abused, or violated. Help us to understand the gift of sex and sexuality as holy.

Litany

Leader: Like artists and sculptors, we appreciate the exquisite design of our bodies and of our sexuality. We rejoice over the gift of sexuality as we embody God's sacred beauty within.

People: **You are the potter, and we are the clay: your marvelous works within us include the elegance of sexual love and desire, given to us by you for the edification of your people.**

Leader: We rejoice in gladness, for we can interact as sacred and sexual beings, not lusting for who we cannot be, not envying others' sacredness or sexuality.

People: **Give us a sense of awe, that we might appreciate every sexual part of our bodies. Make us holy as we bathe and dress, respectful of each and every erogenous zone of each of our bodies.**

Leader: O Holy Spirit, anoint us with discernment so that we may not engage in sexual practices at the wrong time or the wrong place, with the wrong person, or for the wrong and sinful reasons.

People: **As beings called out by you to serve and love, we thank you for our sexuality and commit to honor this gift as you have honored us in the giving of graced passion.**

Benediction

May you go to serve the Lord as a sacred, sexual being. May you practice wisdom, respect, and delight for the joys of sexuality. May you go forth, never taking your sexuality for granted, releasing all shame, guilt, and lust. God be with you always; go now in peace. Amen.

—ɱ—

29. Family/Ancestors

Beware lest there be among you a man or woman or family
or tribe, whose heart turns away this day from the Lord our
God to go and serve the gods of those nations; lest there
be among you a root bearing poisonous and bitter fruit.
—Deuteronomy 29:18

Quotation

Everybody understands . . . as much as anyone can understand another's pain . . . but you've . . . you've forgotten to
be polite. . . . Blacks concede that burrowing, jibing, jiv-
ing, signifying, disrespecting, cursing, even outright insults might
be acceptable under particular conditions, but aspersions cast
against one's family call for immediate attack." (Maya Angelou,
author, professor, poet, musician, performer)

Invocation

Creator, Parent of us all, as we come to worship, we rejoice that
you created the world, you created us, and you created families
and communities. As we gather to praise you, strengthen the ties
that bind us, help us celebrate each other as neighbor, help us
love each other as friend.

Reflections

Families come in all sizes, shapes, and colors. For some, family
represents kinships based on blood relations. Some experience
family as a tight network of loving friends. Some have extended
families made up of blood relations and cousins ten times
removed, coworkers, church members, and friends who share

common interests. Many define family as a group of people living under one roof and usually under the guidance of one or
two adults. In ancient Israel, kinship groups included families,
tribes, clans, and nations. With more mobility, many of us no
longer live in the same community where we grew up, so we
have created families, groups of people who share similar values. Some of us have been blessed with terrific, nurturing, loving families who helped us soar and become loving and
creative. Some of us were born into dysfunctional families,
environments where we were not loved, perhaps not even tol-
erated, where there was addiction and abuse, where we were
not understood, and where no one paid attention to us. Some
of us were abandoned. The pain was so great that all that we
could do was lash out and hurt others until we were incarcerated. Today, we have an opportunity to model "family" to others. Family can be two adults, one adult with children, two
adults with children, grandparents and children, blended
groups, extended families of aunts, uncles, cousins, those we
have adopted, those we have embraced though there is no biological connection. Family can be roommates who love,
respect, and support each other as friends. By God's grace you
can create a family, a group of kindred spirits who love you just
as you are.

Prayer

Beloved God, you have given us an opportunity to be in community on an intimate level, and we celebrate our ties and connections. You have given us people with whom we can share
special occasions: births and baptisms, youthful rites of passage,
graduations, weddings, special honors, and funerals. We give
thanks for this institution of "the family"—for biological,
adopted, extended, and play families in which we are molded,
shaped, nurtured, educated, and loved. We give special thanks
for those families who have formally or informally nurtured and
adopted us, or who opened their hearts to us. We give thanks for
the lives of those who were separated from their families and died

through the Middle Passage to this country, and for our ancestors who survived Middle Passage, allowing us to be here today. For great grandparents, for grandparents, for nanas and papas, for mothers and fathers, for aunts and uncles, for sisters and brothers, for godparents, for cousins, for nieces and nephews—for all those relatives whom we know, and for those we have never known, we give thanks. Help us have the courage to step in and call a halt to any and all varieties of abuse, to better educate adults in parenting, to better communicate and resolve conflict. Thank you for family.

Litany

Leader: Glory, glory, how beautiful to be surrounded by family, by people who share ancestry, commitment, and love, who are called by God to be family.

People: **We rejoice and pause as we realize the awesome responsibility of being family, the hard work involved in building relationships, and the patience and care required.**

Leader: In God's blessed assurance, we pray for the ability to listen well to the physical, mental, emotional, and spiritual needs of our loved ones, and to respond in love.

People: **Let us always have the courage to support family members in ways that are responsible and true. Help us say no to that which is hurtful, and yes to that which saves.**

Leader: Let us honor the children, youth, adults, and senior members of our families, according them all respect, dignity, support, nurture, safety, and care.

People: **In faith and humility, we pledge to take seriously**

101

our family commitments, creating balance in our relationships and remembering the gift of family.

Benediction

As we go forth to love and serve God, may we go about ministry as family. May the lives we live today honor God, our ancestors, and ourselves. May we be a family of covenant faith, as the light of the love within brings us together in joy and thanksgiving. God be with you always; go now in peace. Amen.

—m—

30. Prison

Remember those who are in prison, as though in prison with them; and those who are ill-treated, since you also are in the body.
—Hebrews 13:3

Quotation

Many people are unaware of the fact that jail and prison are two entirely different institutions. People in prison have already been convicted. Jails are primarily for pretrial confinement, holding places until prisoners are either convicted or found innocent. More than half of the jail populations have never been convicted of anything, yet they languish in these cells. . . . Jails and prisons are designed to break human beings, to convert the population into specimens in a zoo . . . obedient to our keepers, but dangerous to each other." (Angela Davis, writer, political activist, educator)

Invocation

We enter into worship aware of the many kinds of jails and prisons, and those who dwell within them. We come into God's presence with thanksgiving and prayers for those behind bars.

Reflections

At the beginning and end of our day, for those of us who are free and not incarcerated, our lives are usually about blessing and possibility. At the beginning and the end of all things is relationship, but those in prison have experienced a deep brokenness. Many prisoners have been victims of sexual abuse, drug- or alcohol-addicted parents, a failed school system, or a lack of religious community. Often when the child was in need no adult was there to fill that need. In prison, one is on a schedule, gets "three hots and a cot," and lives a regimented existence. Some people in prison should not be incarcerated. Some were at the wrong place at the wrong time. Others could not afford basic legal representation and were railroaded because of poverty, ignorance, and weak family support systems. Some people in prison intentionally committed heinous crimes and need to be behind bars. We are called to remember that attending to inmates is a ministry, and there may be possibility for change. God and God's children are dynamic, living beings. God is ever steadfast and sure, but God embraces change just as God embraces loving us. No matter how difficult a situation appears, we must never lose hope. *Are we sick and tired to the point that we are paralyzed? Or, Are we sick and tired to the point that we are determined not to be sick of mind and spirit?* The church has an obligation to minister to those in prison, to be a sanctuary, a refuge for children, youth, and adults in need, offering an alternative for them before they get into the system. Who will go and work with those imprisoned?

Prayer

From within prison walls, both actual and symbolic, we call out to you, gracious Yahweh, to ask for forgiveness and for the blessedness of your salvation. Some of us have committed awful wrongs and are serving time. Some of us are in such pain that while, we are not in a jail cell, our hearts and spirits are deeply wounded and troubled. We are in a prison of estrangement from your blessedness. Help us feel your presence and a spirit of freedom until we are no longer enslaved. We also pray that all of your children throughout the world experience freedom and peace: freedom from sin or broken relationships with you and others; freedom from hunger and thirst; freedom from homelessness and addictions; and freedom from all oppression. With your freedom, we know deliverance. Your deliverance provides refuge during raging storms and in lockdowns, helps us transcend the grief of loss, shame, and pain, and move us from misery to delight in you. We love you, for you have given us the gift of life. Even in prison, we thank you for turning our mourning into dancing, and our slavery into things of freedom.

Litany

Leader: Like Paul and Silas, who were unjustly imprisoned, we know that many behind prison bars should be in treatment facilities where they can get love and support.

People: **For those who are in prison for crimes they committed, we recognize that many of them are there because family and society did not protect them and provide them with encouragement, time, and love during their formative years.**

Leader: For those in prison, we pray for God's mercy. For those who have done violence to others, we pray that they may come to realize the error of their ways, and make peace with themselves about their plight.

People: **For all people hurting and in pain, those who are imprisoned outside of prison walls, we offer prayer**

for their uplift, that they may know transformation and peace.

Leader: For the families of those who are incarcerated, we pray for strength and peace. Even when we do not understand why people behave the way they do, we can love them for who they are and who God created them to be.

People: **We honor the labors of those who work for justice. We pray that those in power understand this position as a privilege and do not abuse the authority of their office but do their best to bring dignity and respect for all persons.**

Benediction

As our time is ended together, as we go out into the world to spread a message of love and concern, let us remember all of those in prison, inside and out. God be with you always; go now in peace. Amen.

31. Class

We are not commending ourselves to you again but giving you cause to be proud of us, so that you may be able to answer those who pride themselves on [one's] position [or class status] and not on [one's] heart.
—2 Corinthians 5:12

Quotation

I find it interesting that the meanest life, the poorest existence, is attributed to God's will, but as human beings become more affluent, as their living standard and style begin to ascend the material scale, God descends the scale of responsibility at a commensurate speed." (Maya Angelou, Renaissance woman, poet, educator, historian, best-selling author, actor, playwright, Civil Rights activist, producer, and director)

Invocation

Blessed Creator, as we come to praise and adore you, gather our hearts beyond our differences of personal, social, and economic status that we might worship in a spirit of unity and thanksgiving. Let us worship God!

Reflections

Many times when we think about societal problems, we quickly contemplate matters of race and sometimes we consider gender, but we often forget about the reality of class as a marker of difference. Class is a way people define social groupings based on social relations, how people make money, how they determine what is important to them, their access to power, cultural privilege, and status in the community. We can figure out persons' class by determining where they attended school, their occupation, what they consider to be recreational or cultural events, how they dress, and what parts of society they have access to. Money is not the only determinant of class, though it is significant. How one relates to travel, vacations, geography, and history; the amount of exposure one has had to cultural activities like music, art, books, theater, and museums; and how one is able to make connections between facts learned are all related to one's class. How one uses verbal and body language is based on social relationships, which are indicators of class. One's class does not make one more intellectual or morally superior. Class happens to be one indicator of how people relate to the world and is quite complicated. Rich people can be poor in spirit, and poor people can be rich in finding joy in life despite their circumstances. Both rich and poor can be victims. One's class status does not indicate how hard one works. Poor people often work incredibly hard for little money. God does not love us more or less because of class. This category of potential and possible discrimination, which we designate as "class," is devised by human beings. God loves each of us unconditionally, not as members of a "class." What's in our pocketbooks, who we know, and what we have access to are irrelevant.

Prayer

Most noble and loving God of power and generosity, bless us to see you in every individual we meet, regardless of what they wear, the accent in their voice, or the price tag of their car. As we are called to do justice, love mercy, and have loving spirits, anoint us with the ability not to be so persuaded by people's credentials that we cannot see who they really are. We thank you for the many gifts of life, including the access to language, fine foods, and culture. We pray for those who have not been so blessed to have material things, but who have stood steadfastly with you and with their communities. Please bless all of those who have wealth and have large hearts, who give generously to help those in need. Please anoint all of those who have access to power.

May they see that power as a place of responsible stewardship. Such power is a gift, not to be confused with personal privilege. Give those of us who can vote and determine those who come to power the gifts of discernment to vote and promote with clear minds, looking for the best leadership for society and not regarding personal gain. Give all of those in leadership positions a sense of well-being, so that they do not have to rule in chaos or oppression, but in justice and generosity. Help us be mindful that we are a community and that we should neither envy those who appear to have more material possessions, nor condemn those who appear to have less. May our hearts remain open to loving our neighbor, not for what they have or lack, or for what they can or cannot do for us.

Litany

Leader: Most honorable Creator, help us express gratitude for all those we meet, that we might not let the trappings of class separate them or us from your love.

People: **Knowing that the first shall be last and the last shall be first, bless us to raise the awareness of our churches and larger communities to always treat each other with dignity.**

Leader: Whether rich or poor, educated or illiterate, talented or mediocre, churched or unchurched, we are all your children; none is superior or inferior for we all belong to you.

People: **Bless us with a pride in the reality of your generosity and your rule over us; give us discerning power so that we will not be trapped by exalted pride in material things and in positions accorded us in this life.**

Leader: Whether rich or poor in goods or spirit, no place in life can offset the guilt we feel when we bring harm to our neighbor, and therefore, harm to the beauty of creation.

People: **May gifts, privilege, position, and accomplishments never separate us from our true selves, from the love of Christ Jesus, and from the anointing power of the Holy Spirit.**

Benediction

In our journeys, in places of high esteem or the streets of the ghetto, let us ever go forth to praise God, to be the light of Christ to others, and to bring the gospel of peace. God be with you always; go now in peace. Amen.

—⟋𝔪⟍—

32. Gender

Your eye is the lamp of your body; when your eye is sound, your whole body is full of light; but when it is not sound, your body is full of darkness.
—Luke 11:34

Quotation

Gender equality is more than a goal in itself. It is a pre-condition for meeting the challenge of reducing poverty, promoting sustainable development and building good governance." (Kofi Annan, United Nations Secretary General)

Invocation

Creator God, as we gather in your Holy Place to offer praise and adoration to you, bring our hearts together as we appreciate the unique createdness of women and men and boys and girls, all of the human family, the family of God. Let us worship God!

Reflections

When we think about describing newborn babies, one of the first questions people ask is, "Is it a girl or a boy?" We think of babies in terms of their gender designation to the point that if the baby has on blue, we assume the baby is a boy; if dressed in pink, then we presume it is a girl. What do we really know about what it means to be boys and girls, to be male and female? Progressive female scholars emphasized the term "gender" to call attention to the sociocultural, sexual differences between male and female. Until the 1970s, the term "man" or "mankind" was understood to include "women." Yet, when the Declaration of Independence was penned, the phrase "all *men* are created equal" pertained explicitly only to white, Anglo-Saxon, Protestant *male* landowners. If you were any other religious/racial/ethnic persuasion, or if you did not own land, then you were not included in the "all *men* are created equal." When we speak of gender we note that there is a great deal of weight behind whether one is classed with the women or the men, particularly when it comes to social position. Much of what we deem male and female traits has been devised as social norms. There is much for scientists to uncover concerning the depths of the biological and physiological distinctions between male and female. There is probably more of a continuum regarding gender categorization, as opposed to polar categories of male and female. At present, many persons consider the designations of female, male, bisexual, transgendered, lesbian, and gay as markers of their gender, their sexuality. Because God made each of us, it behooves all of us not to judge or condemn persons' full understanding of who they are. Perhaps all persons will then receive equal respect in all avenues of life and vocation and receive equal pay for equal work.

Prayer

Tender, loving, compassionate God, how marvelous is your handiwork for all generations. Only a God like you could have created us so much like you, in your image, and yet so different from each other in gender and sexuality. How like you to create humanity in the expansive and beautiful manner that you created the lilies, and roses, and daffodils, and birds of paradise of the fields. You gave us different colors, sentiments, ways of expressing, ways of being. Bless us to honor you by being tolerant of our brothers and sisters. Help us to not fear the beauty of differences in gender, but to embrace the difference. Bless us to see the importance of honoring all people and living with dignity, treating no one as inferior because of their gender designation. Help us release the need to be judgmental, fearful, and bitter whenever ambiguity seems to be in our midst. Anoint us with the love that connects our communities to become the body of Christ you so desire us to be. When we are confused and feel misunderstood regarding our bodies, our minds, our gender, and how these categories affect who we are and the call you have upon our lives, surround us with your love. Please send us an angel of mercy who can minister to us and make our way plain.

Litany

Leader: We give thanks for the gift of diversity God has created as we live our lives as gendered persons, grateful for the gift of creation.

People: **Blessed be God who, in making heaven and earth, made us sacred beings who wear the cloak of gender as we go out to spread the gospel.**

Leader: As we enjoy the close of day, we think about how blessed we are to be created in the *Imago Dei*, as male

111

or as female, and of the continuums betwixt and between.

People: **Blessed be all of God's children, so wonderfully and beautifully made, exquisite as diamonds, radiant as gold, in bodies large and small, with voices deep and high, as gendered beings, grateful for life itself.**

Leader: In the springs and autumns, the summers and winters of our lives, help us appreciate all of the aspects that make us human. Help us be faithful to witness to you as gendered creatures who have the gifts of feeling and thinking.

People: **Blessed are you, most generous Creator, for you did not create us as robots, but fashioned us through spirit, body, gender, and other distinctive characteristics that bring us joy and pleasure. Blessed are you, O holy and noble God.**

Benediction

As the hour of our praise has ended, let us go forth enfleshed as gendered beings who know the gifts of grace, mercy, commitment, love, and service. God be with you always; go now in peace. Amen.

33. Leadership

*"I know your works, your love and faith and service and patient
endurance, and that your latter works exceed the first."*
—Revelation 2:19

Quotation

Despite widespread cynicism concerning leadership in our
society, we still can be moved by the presence of authentic moral guidance. . . . Transformational leadership
engages with others so that the leader and followers "raise one
another to higher levels of motivation and morality. . . .
Authentic leaders are like diamonds who typically exist in the
rough, their value and potential unrecognized by most people."
(Robert M. Franklin, President, Interdenominational
Theological Center; administrator, scholar, preacher)

Invocation

Children of God, let us make our hearts, minds, spirits, and
bodies ready to receive the blessings and good news of redemptive life and healthy leadership! Let us worship God!

Reflections

Leadership and leadership development have become buzzwords
over the last two decades, buzzwords crucial to our understanding
of all sorts of programs and commitments in the twenty-first century. A leader is a person who guides and conducts, one who has
commanding authority or influence. A leader presides over various bodies, from religious to governmental organizations, to offer
wisdom and instruction. A leader is one who has a vision for what
a group needs to be doing and how the group can best accomplish
its goals, missions, vision, and dreams. A leader is one who has the
capacity to lead—to be in charge, direct, go ahead of, steer, show

the way. Leadership is ministry done to uplift the constituents and the person in charge. Some think leadership is only about personal aggrandizement. Others think that leadership concerns self-sacrifice and doing without for some higher purpose. Perhaps leadership—balanced, healthy, collaborative, innovative leadership—is somewhere in the middle. Leadership done well is an opportunity for all participants to grow, for focus to be obtained, for insignificant matters to be unearthed and resolved, and for the primary agenda to be strategically placed up front. Leadership is an experience of contributing and being contributed to; it moves us outside the box, calls us to work smarter not harder. Such leadership does not sacrifice everything for fame. Fame can be a part of superb leadership, but it cannot become the idol.

Prayer

God, you created all leaders, fashioned an Abraham and Sarah, a Moses and Zipporah, a Priscilla and Aquilla. We come in gratitude, fear, and trembling, recognizing the awesome responsibility that comes with leadership, especially leadership in our church and local communities. We come in gratitude, for we were chosen as leaders and see this opportunity to serve as a blessing. We come in fear or awe of you, the One graced in love and power. We come in fear, for the task seems so large. We come trembling because of the weight of such leadership. We come humbled and honored. We pray that our humility will never be an excuse not to persevere, but that we will know joy and anticipation. As leaders, we pray to have wisdom in our decision making, to have courage in making hard choices, and to have dignity in the office from which we operate as leaders called by God.

Litany

Leader: Standing on the promises of God, we recognize the gifts of leadership and responsibility, the sacredness of the office, and the privilege of being so elected or appointed.

People: **We honor the goodness of creation and of the Creator who sustains us as we stand in God's marvelous universe, the place where we perform the duties of good leaders and good followers.**

Leader: Standing on the promises of God, we accept the call of leadership, as both lay and clergy, to spread the gospel, and to witness to new life and the option for change.

People: **We honor the earth and the fullness thereof; as we make our homes here, we build partnerships here and follow divine and human leadership here.**

Leader: Standing on the promises of God, we recommit our bodies, spirits, and minds to excellence in leadership; even when tired, we will be open to learn and exercise better leading.

People: **Holy, holy, holy is God. Holy is the work we are called to, for we are made in God's image. May we embrace a sense of the holy when we lead and follow in mercy, justice, humility, courage, and joy.**

Benediction

And now that our hour for worship has ended, we leave, sharing the blessedness of leadership, from mountaintop to valley, from corporate suite to corner store! God be with you always; go now in peace. Amen.

—ᗯ—

34. Politics/Power

Death and life are in the power of the tongue,
and those who love it will eat its fruits.
—Proverbs 18:21

Quotation

I enter the discussion of authority with the understanding that authority is legitimated power or shared power. The traditional concept of power is a natural consequence of an authoritarian model of obedience based on submission. The world is separated into entities with little or no interrelationship. Power becomes the property of these separated entities and is identified with domination. This notion of power involves the notion of invulnerability. The concept of power that comes from decision and responsibility is one that entails the ability to effect change and to work with others." (Emilie Townes, professor, scholar, minister, social ethicist)

Invocation

Come now before God, recognizing that power and politics is a part of our lives that should not be feared, but prayerfully entered into. As God is the giver of power, let us come in power to worship!

Reflections

Understanding the detailed workings of power, the related critical issues, and how the use of power can turn back on itself is complex. With all of the complexities of the use and manipulation of power, it is most necessary to deal with power when doing ministry. When we think about the word power, we think of words like wealth, envy, status, fame, hard work, connections, timing, and privilege. Power concerns the ability to act or produce an effect, to have a sense of authority. Legally, power concerns official or governmental authority, capacity, or right. In the world of sports, power pertains to physical might, strength, efficiency, and skill. Power is not inherently good or demonic. Having power can be the result of inheritance, accumulation of wealth, political or priestly office, or connections with a given community that bestows a certain amount of authority and privilege on an individual or group of people. When power becomes manipulative and exclusive, many get hurt and do without. Power, however, is not the enemy, by definition. The power to do, to make a difference is God-given power.

Prayer

Listening, loving God, in our comings and goings, we often have access to power, and we often deal with it inappropriately. Our grasp of power often stagnates and becomes incestuous because we refuse to share it. Power not shared becomes a sickness. Sometimes we rule by chaos and confusion to keep those who work with us and for us at cross-purposes. Sometimes we even place our souls and minds on the market for sale. Discerning God, please help us see when our use of power becomes idolatrous and dampens our connections with you, the catalyst for all power. Help us see power as a tool for building community, and for making a difference. Help us be mindful of those who are less fortunate, understanding that poverty is not romantic, but a symptom of systemic idolatry and greed. Bless those who are poor and without access to power. Help governments everywhere become more accountable and more empathetic with those who are marginalized, and who are named other. Because wealth and poverty occupy the same place in the absence of love, we pray for the wisdom to always use our resources to honor you, love all, and be a true neighbor.

Litany

Leader: We give thanks for the many kinds of power we have at our disposal. We pray to have the understanding and good reasoning to take the authority to lead with justice and respect.

People: **How blessed we are to be able to exercise power and to have the clarity to know when power is being manipulated to cause harm.**

Leader: We pray that all persons with the authority to exercise power will be respectful of children and of older persons, gleaning from their experience, ever mindful to never oppress or discount someone because of age.

People: **How blessed we are to be able to relate to people of different age groups and to handle our power intergenerationally with dignity and justice.**

Leader: We pray that persons with the authority to exercise power will be respectful to all persons with so-called handicapping conditions, appreciating the gift of health and the realities of diversity regarding mental, emotional, physical, and spiritual health.

People: **We are grateful for different gifts, different life experiences, and for the offerings that varied persons bring with them. May we practice judiciousness and grace when we have the opportunity to have power and make decisions that affect our lives and the lives of others.**

Benediction

Beloveds, go now in peace, with an attitude of gratitude and a sense of humility as we go into the world exercising the various gifts, graces, and powers given us by God. God be with you always; go now in peace. Amen.

35. Protest

But they shook off the dust from their feet [in protest]
against them, and went to Iconium.
—Acts 13:51

Quotation

I f you will protest courageously, and yet with dignity and
Christian love, when the history books are written in future
generations, the historians will have to pause and say, 'There
lived a great people . . . a Black people . . . who injected new
meaning and dignity into the veins of civilization." (Martin
Luther King, Jr. [1929–1968], pastor, Civil Rights activist,
author)

Invocation

As we enter this consecrated place of God, we come to worship,
to protest the times when we forget to praise God, and to celebrate the moment-to-moment connection God maintains with
us!

Reflections

When societal or ecclesial crises arise, instead of envisioning
protest, some will think, "let's go back to the good old days, to
the way we used to do things." First, there never was any such
reality as "the good old days." We tend to romanticize the past
and have selective memories and foci. Do we wish to return
to the days of no antibiotics, inside plumbing, or telephones;
to the days of slavery, to the decimation of our Native
American population, to Japanese American internment

camps?[1] Do we want to entertain the times when women routinely died in childbirth and children routinely died of communicative diseases before the age of five? We are where we are. This is not to romanticize contemporary life in these United States and act as if we do not have problems. There are problems with drugs and crime and violence. Much of this country was founded on violence, and we have always had drugs. Yet, there were more alcoholics and opium and heroin addicts in this country during the early 1900s than there are in the twenty-first century. Our current "War on Drugs" calls for a protest shaped and orchestrated by love and sharing of time and resources. Teens and adults often get into trouble as a corollary to a troubled childhood. There continues to be the need to protest social injustice—to protect our civil rights, to fight against toxic waste, and to challenge practices that lead to environmental and cultural pollution. We must engage in proactive protest, realizing that inside every adult is a child waiting to be loved. Inside every child or adult is something sacred.

Prayer

Blessed God, even when situations seem hopeless and we feel that we cannot make a difference, we pray that we will not run away, or get too focused on our personal problems, but that we will be able to take a stand, to protest against injustice and wrongdoing. Our soul longs for you as we stand against difficulty. We desire that our relationship with you be the center of our lives, the anchor and altar of our lives that will enable us to object to inequity and

---

1. We should note that more than fifteen hundred persons of Japanese extraction, who were residing in countries in Central and South America, were rounded up by the FBI and extradited to the United States by those countries collusively, for confinement in "detention centers" [i.e., American "concentration camps"], despite their being citizens of those countries. They were held as hostages for exchange to Japan during World War II in return for Japan's release of American P.O.W.s. Their "hostage" status was denied for more than fifty years by the United States government.

miscarriages of justice. We honor you as the Potter, the Refiner, the Architect of the universe to us, the straw, clay, and bricks. We stand to be molded to protest any harm that comes to our neighbor. Grant us mercy. For though the enemies without and those inside wage war against us, yet do we trust in you, for you have shown us the importance of doing protest ministry on behalf of others. Though our tears pour forth, we are not ashamed. These are tears of joy and hope that flow out of our struggles, our protests, and our accomplishments by faith, as manifestations of your grace. When day is done, we lay our heads to rest in your faithful love, knowing that we have lived this day well. We protested for the sake of justice and love for ourselves and our communities.

Litany

Leader: Gracious, loving God, hear our call, and let us not suffer alone. Awaken us to your noble vision of abundance and justice for us; be with us as we protest so that all may know health and joy.

People: **Creator God, we thank you for your gifts of salvation that bring us toward balance and a sense of the sacred, despite times of difficulty, misunderstandings, and trouble.**

Leader: Gracious, loving God, do not forsake us, but surround us with your steadfast love, your mercy, and your divine discernment, that we may see through smoky clouds and windows clearly, knowing when to stand firm, and when to compromise or protest.

People: **Creator God, as your children, we rejoice in your righteousness and hasten to confess our desire to transcend all social injustice and our own shortcomings; help us to be gracious even at the door of terror and indecision.**

Leader: Lead us, guide us, and protect us as we journey

through the valleys and shadows of protest, life, and death. Redeem us in our comings and our goings as we pledge our faith, hope, and trust in you.

People: **For the blessings of peace and benevolent joy, for the redemption of all creation, we give you the praise, the glory, the blessings in prayer and covenant faith.**

Benediction

Sisters and brothers, leave now, remembering what you have learned, that you are called to protest wrong and injustice, called to live a righteous life. God be with you always; go now in peace. Amen.

—⁓—

36. Race

That you may eat and drink at my table in my kingdom, and sit on thrones judging the twelve tribes [races] of Israel.
—Luke 22:30

Quotation

Long before [1986] . . . I had begun to feel that public discussion of the race issue had become virtually choreographed. Blacks were expected to speak on tones of racial entitlement, to show a modified black power assertiveness . . . not as strident as the sixties black power rhetoric, but certainly not ameliorative as the integrationist tone of the civil rights era. Racism had to be offered as the greatest barrier to black progress, and blacks themselves had still to be seen primarily as racial victims. Whites, on the other hand, had both to show concern and a measure of befuddlement at how other whites could still be racist. There also had to be in whites a clear deference to the greater racial authority of blacks, whose color translated into a certain racial expertise. If there was more than one black, whites usually receded into the [background] while the black 'experts' argued. This is still the standard media formula, the ideal choreography of black and white." (Shelby Steele, scholar, research fellow)

Invocation

God of many nations, many peoples, many tribes, many races pour down your Spirit upon us, so that as we gather, we can celebrate and honor the gift of our diversities and the distinctions of our similarities; as we come together as one, we gather to worship you.

Reflections

In a world that has so many different cultures, and peoples, and ways of being, it almost seems impossible that we can get along, given the amount of animosity that festers around ethnicity and race. Is there a way for us to coexist fully? Race is a sociocultural construction, not a biological one, that exists for the purpose of economic and political domination. History tells us that we cannot live side by side in peace. Human beings destroy each other: think about the deaths and the destruction of Kosovo and the former Yugoslavia, Rwanda, Ireland, the bombings throughout the 1990s, and the plane crashes on September 11 into the World Trade Center, the Pentagon, and the Pennsylvania countryside—to the ancient, medieval, romantic, and modern eras' heinous crimes of conquest, genocide, molestation, and tortures that occurred in the Crusades, the Holocaust, the Middle Passage, the Trail of Tears, and on and on. From a microcosmic perspective, every day the media in the United States reports of crimes against women and children, against those deemed minority, particularly those labeled other. In some ways, everyone is "other" when she or he is disconnected from God. With a greater awareness of self in relationship through faith, and the celebration of difference—

whether that is a difference of class, gender, sexual persuasion, or race—one experiences a new kind of power.

Prayer

Ever faithful God, who hears, helps, heals, and makes us feel and look different, we honor your blessed wonder that connects all living things. Help us accept that everyone is our neighbor, sister, and brother, whether their skin be brown, black, white, red, or yellow. Help us experience difference expressed as race as the many colors and types of flowers in a garden. Help us grow beyond stereotypes, arrogance, victimhood, and fear. Give peace to those who are ill and distressed, who are ashamed of their racial/ethnic background. Help make our churches and society conscious of the needs of the many as well as of the few, of those who dominate and those who tend to be oppressed. Broaden our horizons that we might desire to learn more about people of different races and belief systems, for the sake of your glory and our own well-being. Let our envy be transformed into excellence, that we might care more about living the right way, instead of being angry at our neighbors for looking different. Let our anger be changed into active love, and help us not confuse our fears around race with our obsession around sex. May our hate be transformed into a hunger for living a righteous life and building healthy communities. May our pain be transformed into your peace that passes all understanding.

Litany

Leader: Creator of peoples of many colors, hues, shapes, cultures, voices, and experiences, show us the splendor of the myriad ways you have created us, like millions of different flowers all blooming in the garden called earth.

People: **Blessed quietness, holy quietness, help us release our fears and hypocrisy that cause us to shun, hate, and stereotype people who look, act, and thus often** think differently from us, and who experience culture in distinctive ways.

Leader: In our own foolishness and need to control, some of us have chosen to dominate others, placing greed and power above generosity and the preservation of life. Grant us the wisdom to see your image in all people, that we may honor the sacred within them.

People: **As we go about our daily lives, teach us to live together honoring your vision of life where there are many races, many ethnicities, many languages, many ways to look, be, think, communicate, learn, teach, govern, and rule.**

Leader: Help us learn that you, gracious God, did not create race; you created people who look different and who have experienced you in unique ways. Help us, who have been oppressed because of our race, learn of ways in which we have internalized this oppression.

People: **God of healing and life, help us not become victims because others treat us harshly. Help us be proud of our skin color, shape of nose, and lips; help us see the beauty in the many colors within our own race, so that we can begin to heal.**

Benediction

As we prepare to depart, help us stand tall and be proud that you chose to create us to look the way we do; may we honor your choices of skin color, body shape, language, and culture for all of your children, as all are part of your created order. God be with you always; go now in peace. Amen.

—〰—

37. Blessing

Jabez called on the God of Israel, saying, "Oh that thou wouldst bless me and enlarge my border, and that thy hand might be with me, and that thou wouldst keep me from harm so that it might not hurt me!" And God granted what he asked.
—1 Chronicles 4:10

Quotation

Thanksgiving and praise of God for all one's many blessings is an integral element in African American worship. That black Americans can praise God after all they have gone through in America is a miracle. That black people have been blessed in America is also a great blessing." (Carlyle Fielding Stewart III, pastor)

Invocation

Now is the time to worship God, the One who created all blessing, the One we are called to bless. Rejoice, be of good cheer; open up for an experience of power and thanksgiving. Let us worship God!

Reflections

Several years ago, the television drama, *The Equalizer*, recounted the stories of an ex-government operative who helped people in difficult, often life-threatening situations, when they had no where else to turn. Sometimes we act like God is an Equalizer: we only go to God as a last ditch effort, when we are desperate and out of options. The God of faith, love, and health is a God who desires relationship long before we get into crisis, a God who blesses us mightily. This God, who made us and loves us, is available for us throughout our lives. This God, as midwife, architect, nurse, and guide, sustains and keeps us. God desires relationship and input into our lives when things are calm as well as when they are in crisis. God's love is unconditional. God does not play the game of take-away. Even when displeased with us, God never withdraws God's love from us. Love is the willingness to show compassion, nurture, care, and concern, the willingness to listen and allow another to be who God created them to be. God, a willing Potter who shapes and loves us in freedom, allows us the gift of freedom to choose.

Prayer

Gracious God, how marvelous are your dwelling places where we can know wholeness, inspiration, and blessing. We come at this time with anticipation and joyous thoughts of coming into your total blessedness and well-being. As we walk amid unknown paths, dangers, and snares, we are yet faithful to our covenant with you. Bless us as individuals and as communities, that we might reflect your goodness and mercy in our relationships and the work of our hands. In our journeys throughout life, when we know not where to go and what to do, your faithful blessedness sustains us. As the Creator and Nurturer of our faith, we look to you and you alone as the source that can bring blessed harmony in our lives. We confess to getting confused about our priorities and sometimes failing to place you first. When we worship, as individuals and communities, strengthen our focus, and help us to be a blessing to others. As we plan and live out our faith, we embrace the possibilities, the hopes, the blessings, and the dreams you gave the prophets of old. In the newness of this day, we open our hearts to be stirred by the blessed outpouring of the Holy Spirit.

Litany

Leader: The blessedness of salvation is a gift of tremendous freedom and deliverance from guilt and loss of friend-

127

ship or love. Blessings restore us to wholeness and relationships.

People: **This freedom releases us from the control of persons, any arbitrary power or restrictions, and brings us into relationship with God.**

Leader: Blessing is a gift of God that provides protection and care; blessing is lived grace that helps us live in freedom and vitality.

People: **The freedom that comes with salvation is grace, a grace that blesses us and blesses God. In the process of blessing us, God cloaks us in love.**

Leader: In response, we engage in worship and responsible living; we bless and honor God as we live our lives, mindful of the call on our lives to live as neighbor in prayer.

People: **Blessing gives us the courage to make confession, to get help, and to make amends for the wrongs we have committed. In so living out our lives we come to know God's loving, salvific grace.**

Benediction

The time for formal celebration is complete, the time to go out and share the good news of the gospel and the awesome reality of God's blessing is upon us. Go in peace to be blessed and be a blessing. God be with you always; go now in peace. Amen.

—〰—

38. Creation

"And to the angel of the church in Laodicea write: 'The words of the Amen, the faithful and true witness, the beginning of God's creation.' "
—Revelation 3:14

Quotation

If God, as DuBois stated, created all reality for equality in electoral representation and wealth's control, then black theology must deepen further the relationship between white supremacist evil and a theological, political economy. To agree to such equal power, therefore, is to maintain and aid God's sovereignty over each created order on earth." (Dwight Hopkins, scholar, author, theologian, professor)

Invocation

Today is God's day, a creative series of moments in history, a day we shall never see again. Let us rejoice, give thanks, and worship our loving God!

Reflections

Creation, the gift of God that allows all life and all beings, is the reality of all existence. "In the beginning, God . . . ," indicates the source of originality, of the power that empowers us to do all that we can do—to wake up each day and go about our tasks of work, school, church, play. Creation is the sphere of God, wherein we get to do great things or do much harm; it is dynamic, vibrant, cyclical. Ecclesiastes tells us that for everything there is a season. Seasons involve change. Nothing stands still—not us, not time. Ernest Becker noted several years ago that we in the West fear death, and that fear controls our drive to do more, to acquire more, to spend more, especially regarding longevity. Our fear of death drives us to try to defeat death. How ironic that we spend so much energy trying to defeat something that is inevitable. This is not to say that we should not take care of ourselves, that we should not have access to various material possessions and diverse experiences. What is central is that we understand that creation is God's gift to us. As such, we are called to be responsible stewards of this gift. This responsibility includes caring for natural resources, being better stewards of our time, getting appropriate rest, relaxation, food, and nurture. We are also called to be better stewards of our relationships, treating ourselves and our neighbors with respect.

Prayer

Gracious Shepherd of the world, you made us in your image, and you are our haven and our protection. We have tremendous gratitude for the gift of your power in all aspects of life. For the beauty of the earth, the seasons and cycles of life, we give thanks. For wisdom and creativity in science, technology, medicine, and the arts, we know deep gratitude. For the diversity of cultures, and races, and ways of being in the world, we bless and honor you. For the covenants you have made with us and on our behalf, we have undying gratitude. The miracles of your creation that we are privileged to experience each day in ordinary and extraordinary ways fill our souls with joy unceasing. You bless us with food, shelter, clothing, and opportunities for education and entertainment. Help us to be mindful of these blessings, and know that many are not as fortunate. Bless us to see our privilege and the needs of others. Help us give unto you, and to your church, and to our communities in ways that all may know the source of our faith and our gifts. Bless us to bestow favor and honor on all of creation, that others may know we are your anointed.

Litany

Leader: To God be the glory for the creation of such an awesome, balanced planet where we make our home: we have land to plow and live upon, food to eat, water to drink, the sun to keep us warm, the glaciers to keep us cool.

People: **All honor, and praise, and glory are yours, O God of Creation, who loves us and inspires us still, even when we forget to be good stewards of all of the gifts you give us.**

Leader: We rejoice for the birds that sing, for the flowers and for the bees that pollinate them and give us honey, for the fish of the ocean, for the trees that give us shade; we rejoice at your generosity, and we humbly accept our responsibility of stewardship.

People: **We bless you, for blessing us still, for making such wondrous experiences available to us out of love and covenant. Be blessed O God, for you are worthy of praise.**

Leader: The gifts of family, ancestors, adults, and children, are created because of your blessing. Our gratitude is vast, for every person in our family is a miracle. We give thanks.

People: **How marvelous is all of your handiwork. We become overwhelmed at your creation. Sometimes we take all creation for granted. Bless us to have a new awareness. Blessed be your name.**

Benediction

In celebrating the gift of creation, we go now, rejoicing in thanksgiving for who we are, for who you are, for the opportunity for divine relations, and for being a part of this marvelous world of yours! God be with you always; go now in peace. Amen.

39. Creativity

You will be enriched in every way for great generosity, which through us
will produce thanksgiving to God.
—2 Corinthians 9:11

Quotation

For she [Alice Walker] reminded us that Art, and the thought and sense of beauty on which [art] is based, is the province not only of those with a room of their own, or of those in libraries, universities and listening. Renaissances—that creating is necessary to those who work in kitchens and factories, nurture children and adorn homes, sweep streets or harvest crops, type in offices or manage them." (Barbara Christian [1943–2000] literary critic, educator, nonfiction writer)

Invocation

Let us rejoice and be exceedingly glad as we come before the Creator who gives all of us the gifts of creativity, of shaping, of producing, of inventing, and of using simple things and sophisticated processes. Blessed be God and those gathered, as we enter into praise with thanksgiving.

Reflections

Every day we have an opportunity to create. As living beings we are creatures, created beings, made holy by God. Whether doing the simple tasks of making up our beds, or engaging in designing buildings or computer disks, writing poetry and sermons, or arranging a spiritual or composing a gospel song, we are involved in creativity. Whether painting buildings, reading a book, clearing an old field, cooking an exquisite or simple meal, planting a garden, or producing a hybrid flower, we are participating in creativity. Rocket scientists, postal workers, police officers, physicians, airplane attendants, disk jockeys, dancers, tennis players, seamstresses, grandmothers, musicians, nurses, truck drivers, and accountants are all involved in creative processes. Creativity involves the ability or power to create, to bring into existence, to produce through imaginative skill. When we create something, we make it up. To be able to create is a gift to be appreciated and not used to cause harm. What would happen, for example, if computer hackers used their skills in technology to teach children who would otherwise not have an opportunity to learn? What would have happened if someone had stopped and taken the time to help a teenager or young adult channel his or her creativity in a healthy way, preventing them from acting out destructively, which could ultimately result in imprisonment? To express one's creativity in love is to take time to be holy.

Prayer

Most worthy God, in the moments of holiness, as we express our God-given talents, we give thanks for opportunities to bring joy and comfort to others through our gift of creativity. We are honored and blessed to experience the pleasure of inspiration when doing simple tasks or when traveling to see breathtaking places in nature. We give thanks for the wonders of our imagination, for the ability to think, to design, to dream life-changing dreams. Help us dare to make a difference and not fear the mystery and uncertainty that often come with the opportunity to create. Bless us to form relationships where we can engage in creativity together. As we participate in church services, give us the anointing that we may feel your presence and understand that you are in us as we are called to sing, pray, dance, preach, or bring comfort through prophetic imagination. Like the ancient voices of the wise ones, help us to be still long enough that we might experience the quietness, where you whisper to us ideas and projects for strengthening our faith and living that faith day to day. Bring angels, messengers to guide us in the process of learning how to be open to new expressions of creativity as we do our best in the moment of inspiration.

Litany

Leader: In thanksgiving, we acknowledge our gratitude for wisdom and visionary attitudes that bring us closer to God, that help us better appreciate the beauty of the earth.

People: **By grace, we open our eyes to see in new ways; and by faith, we open our minds and hearts to create new things and new ways of being.**

Leader: In joy, we thank God for all of the many acts of creativity that make it possible for us to live life fully and joyfully; may we be willing to collaborate more and to share with others.

People: **In our daily walk, may we become loving, just stewards, taking no more than we need and giving back as much as we are able.**

Leader: In our teaching, preaching, and leadership, may we always embrace opportunities to use our imagination in ways that can better inform and inspire our congregations.

People: **May we be open to change and to new and different ways of worshiping God, as God fixes our hearts and heals our wounds, freeing our imagination and our thoughts for good.**

Benediction

As the light of God shines from east to west, as we honor all of our creative gifts, may we go from this place looking for God's "glimmers of grace," for those sparks of creativity that will help us sustain our community and help those in need. God be with you always; go now in peace. Amen.

—ıw—

40. Forgiveness

And Peter said to them, "Repent, and be baptized every one of you in the name of Jesus Christ for the forgiveness of your sins; and you shall receive the gift of the Holy Spirit."
—Acts 2:38

Quotation

African peoples have always known the great toll that hatred takes on both the personality of individual and the life of the community. In the interest of their highest goal, community, they have shunned hatred by cultivating the virtue of forgiveness through the habitual exercise of kindness." (Peter Paris, scholar, author, professor, Christian ethicist, student of African peoples)

Invocation

Merciful One, we enter into Mount Zion in gratitude and all humility. For your grace and your mercy, let us experience your forgiving, covenantal love as we gather here, offering adoration, praise, and thanksgiving. We bless you for blessing us as we come to you in awe.

Reflections

Hundreds of words in scripture extol the virtue of forgiveness. To ask for forgiveness of our debts to God and others is to bow to

and accept the divine, grace-given virtue of humility. To give forgiveness to others is to follow Jesus' command to love ourselves
by forgiving our debtors. To forgive means to let go of a resent-
ment regarding some act, or to release someone from a claim
where they need to give something in return. In the prayer Jesus
taught his disciples, we rehearse so often "forgive us our trespasses as we forgive those who trespass against us." This condi-
tional claim reminds us that if we do not forgive, we *will not* be
forgiven. One must confess the wrong that one does or that has
been done to oneself. To move from the hurt to quick forgiveness
is cheap, cavalier, and not fully grounded in faith and healing.
Too often some well-meaning individuals try to rush a wounded
person or victim into forgiveness. No one should be badgered
into forgiving something or someone. We can forgive because
God's grace empowers us to do so. There has to be a sense of
safety, support, and trust for one to have the space to acknowledge betrayal. When we fully experience the hurt, we can make
our confession and begin to take steps toward healing. When the
injury to us has healed, then we can be moved to forgive. Some
people have a mountaintop experience and a sense of well-being
comes relatively quickly. For others, the full process of release
and/or healing may take years. With the release comes the space
for forgiveness, for the letting go, for living in sanctuary with
God.

Prayer

Loving, gracious *El Roi*, God of Seeing, we thank you for creating us to be in community, wherein we may experience relationships. In our relationships, we fall short. We hurt each other,
misunderstand words and deeds, become self-centered, and fail
to practice being good neighbors. Your mercy illumines our path
and calls us to forgive those who have harmed us and have done
all manner of evil against us. We utter the words of forgiveness
many times because it is our Christian responsibility. We seek
forgiveness from you and from those we have injured because it

is our Christian duty. What are we to do when the terrible act is so unexplainable that we do not believe it is possible to forgive or be forgiven? What happens when we are so racked with pain and grief that our tongues become heavily laden and we cannot speak when asking for, or wanting to offer forgiveness? Only your comfort and presence can give us the freedom and ability to forgive the unspeakable or ask for forgiveness of the unbearable. Come to us as that "Balm in Gilead" so that we may always yield to you, as you order our steps, bear our burdens, lighten the load, and bring us to a place of peace.

Litany

Leader:　As we walk through the valley of the shadow of grief, pain, and death, anoint us with your blessedness, that we might confess, in preparation for seeking and embracing forgiveness.

People:　**When we harm others, or when others harm us, help us acknowledge the wrongdoing and forgive ourselves and others for our and their mistakes.**

Leader:　Help us not judge others unfairly, so that we will not be judged unjustly by you or by others. Let us live the life of joy and contentment, open to forgiving those who do us harm.

People:　**Help us practice the habits of hospitality and kindness. Melt the hatred in our hearts, so that we may know the peace that comes with the sacrament and testament of forgiving others.**

Leader:　O God of our salvation, deliver us, and forgive us our sins, trespasses, and debts for the sake of righteousness and for your glory, from everlasting to everlasting.

People: In the mystery of forgiveness, let us be your light, your vessel, that others may desire to be in relationships with you, coming to know that indefinable, gentle peace.

Benediction

O righteous One, our strength and shield, cloak us in your bosom of comfort and forgiving love that we may wear life as a loose garment, that we may release the chips off our shoulders. May we come to know you in an intimate way that we might be totally free. God be with you always; go now in peace. Amen.

—w—

41. Glory

"And the glory of the LORD shall be revealed, /and all flesh shall see it together, for the mouth of the LORD has spoken."
—Isaiah 40:5

Quotation

I looked at my hands, to see if I was de same person now I was free. Dere was such a glory ober eberything, de sun came like gold trou de trees, and ober de fields, and I felt like I was in heaven." (Harriet Tubman [1820–1913], U.S. abolitionist, emancipator)

Invocation

As your glory radiates in the heavens and on the earth, in the waters of the deep, in the valleys made low, and upon the mountaintops high, bring us together in prayerful unity, as we come to worship our God!

Reflections

While glory can refer to nature or humanity, the most important use of the biblical notion of glory and majesty concerns God. God's glory is the external manifestation of God's reality through revelation in nature, for example as theophany, as in the burning bush. God's glory can be seen or sensed. Sometimes the glory of God is hidden or concealed from us. God's glory indicates God's presence, as when God was made manifest to Moses in the cloudy pillar and the Mt. Sinai experiences in the book of Exodus. God has glory before any external manifestation occurs. Sometimes one refers to God's glory in recognition of glory's reality, particularly as we engage in praise. The experience of glory is mystical or spiritual. We look up from the thoughts of nothingness, and we know it is God. We know God's glory when we become transformed by grace. When we turn around and really listen to the wind, to a baby's voice, to the sweet melody of an anthem or spiritual, to a solo saxophone or flute, to a violin or cello: when we really, really listen, we know God's glory. We experience God's glory when we first experience an angel of God with melodies, glorious, ever transcending. The first sound that a baby ever makes is a manifestation of God's glory, for with new life, we come to know that hope is being reborn. Our hope can never die, because in that moment, we witness new life, God's glory.

Prayer

Glorious Lord, in the quiet of the midnight, in the dew of morning, in the heat of noonday, and in the setting of the sun, we see your glory. In your majestic creation, you have blessed musicians and composers to create repertoires of galactic anthems, to announce you in the swells and diapasons on great organs, and to conduct great choruses, echoing the thousands of years of praising God: "Hallelujah!" Each time we laugh and cry, you are with us: "Glory, Glory!" As we reach out and proclaim your word to all generations, multitudes will begin to come. Help us come alive as you restore us from hate and distrust. Help us educate the philosophies of ignorance, help us make the welcome table inclusive. As your Spirit broods over the waters and the earth, you dwell in us. As our prayers are lifted up, we glorify your name above all great choruses, preached words, benedictions, and great Amens! Your glory so blesses us that we truly come alive to live love, to let ourselves be changed, and to let go of vengeance and violence.

Litany

Leader: How glorious is your dwelling place, O Lord, who reigns and lives throughout all time, loving us still in the midst of good times and bad, springtime and harvest.

People: **The glory of the Lord appears in clouds, in refining fires, in the great mysterious movement of the Holy Spirit, sanctifying all in view.**

Leader: The glory of the Lord appears throughout time to prophets, to congregations, to those who wait on the Lord and listen for the call upon their lives.

People: **Let us sing and shout; with timbrels and harps; let us clap our hands and dance, proclaiming to all the awesome, loving glory of the God of hosts, the God of earth, and the God of heaven.**

Leader: Holy, holy, holy is our glorious God; heaven and earth are full of God's glory! All honor and glory is yours in this moment, in the past forever gone, and in the future yet to come.

People: **Hosanna in the highest! Blessed by our glorious God! Let Mount Zion rejoice, let the sons and**

daughters of God be glad. Serve God with joy, gladness, and thanksgiving for the blessedness of God's
glory.

Benediction

May the glory of God anoint you with love, peace, and a hopeful vision for a blessed today as we leave our time of worship to
go out and share the message of God's glory! God be with you
always; go now in peace. Amen.

—m—

42. Grace

And God is able to make all grace abound to you,
so that in all things at all times, having all that you need,
you will abound in every good work.
—2 Corinthians 9:8 (NIV)

Quotation

God's grace occur(s) in the here and now of [human] existence. The grace of God is God's judicial act. . . . Grace
is God's power . . . a personified power which works
against the power of sin and takes over its lost command. . . .
The Christian is called to Grace. . . . The grace of God also cor-
responds to that other event in the nature of God namely, the
wrath of God. Grace is the event in which God restores me and
places within my grasp my lost possibility of authentic being.
Grace enables me to be that which God intended for me to be."
(Joseph A Johnson, Jr., Christian Methodist Episcopal bishop,
professor, author, scholar, pulpiteer)

141

Invocation

God of love and power, we come before your presence with eager anticipation, waiting for your grace to fall afresh on us. Gather our thoughts and hearts and spirits in one accord as we begin this graced service of the sung, prayed, and preached Word. We ask for your anointing and the empowerment of the Holy Spirit as we focus on you in this time.

Reflections

Grace is not an abstract thought or design, and it is not a mindless recipe for false piety. Grace, by definition, cannot be static. Grace is multifaceted, at once an attitude, a process, a way of being, and a mighty connecting link between humanity and God. The place of grace is that realm of safety amid trouble, the location where we can yet hold to belief and assurance despite doubts and desperation. Grace is an attitude that lets us persevere even when it seems like we are getting nowhere fast. Grace is a process of being steadfast, even when trapped between a rock and a hard place. The experience of grace is a way of being in the world, a way of looking and holding oneself, ever hopeful, ever intimate with God, holding onto covenant when many things physical, psychological, and financial seem to be problematic. At the same time, a graceful countenance will allow one to be on the offensive and to create proactive strategies, so that one is less prone to fall into self-inflicted despair and difficulty. The living of a graceful covenant provides us not only with a contextual freedom, but also with a vitality that comes with that freedom, a will to live responsibly and make good choices, and a commitment to be open to the awesome blessings of God.

Prayer

Gracious God, we come rejoicing in delight and exceeding joy. In you we find amazing, awesome grace, sweeter than any sound or moment in life. In your grace, we can have peace and joy even when feeling lost. By your grace, we are able to experience the fruits and works of the Spirit. Your grace brings value to our lives and helps us keep your commandments. We bless you for the grace that allows the spreading of the gospel that we experience—your rule or kingdom in our lives. Your grace is so sufficient that it enables the restoration of good relationships. Your grace makes possible joy, love, peace, kindness, patience, generosity, faithfulness, self-control, and gentleness. Blessed One, so great is your gift of grace that it seems impossible for us to thank you enough for this gift. Through faith and grace, Jesus himself lived and suffered for humanity for the sake of joy. We bless you for the graced ministry of Christ that we are called to participate in by being obedient to your grace as participating ministers, disciples, and followers—bringing the good news, praying for the sick and lost, and teaching others to help themselves. As we continue to walk by faith, we bless you for the generosity of your grace, and the joy that abounds to us.

Litany

Leader: Rejoice, rejoice, O people of God! Rejoice for the gifts of grace that sustain us, for the spirituality that integrates us, for the health that lets us move and make a difference in the world.

People: **As people of God, we lift our graced voices in praise and commitment, moving toward being open to other faith communities in love and respect.**

Leader: Rejoice, rejoice, O people of God! Rejoice for opportunities to share the grace of God everywhere you go, to create communities and a world that is safe, to move toward an extraordinary love of God and love of ourselves and our neighbors.

People: As the people of God, we rejoice in the gifts of youth and old age, for each moment is gracious in God's sight; each moment is a time for us to be more Christlike, walking a pathway toward unity amid difference.

Leader: Rejoice and give thanks for the traditions on which we stand, for the author of grace, and for those who need to reform as we grow and serve in this present age.

People: As children of God, we embrace this day as a unique day graced by God. We open ourselves to be blessed and to be a blessing to others. We hold fast to God's love and everlasting grace, the context for our increased spiritual awareness.

Benediction

May the grace of God keep and sustain you. May Christ's peace hold and guide you. May the power of the Holy Spirit anoint you in your going out and your coming in. May the grace that abounds so embrace you that you go forth in love. God be with you always; go now in peace. Amen.

43. Joy

Yet I will rejoice in the LORD, */I will joy in the God of my salvation.*
—Habakkuk 3:18

Quotation

The radically comic character of Afro-American life—the pervasive sense of play, laughter and ingenious humor of blacks—flows primarily from the profound Afro-American Christian preoccupation with the tragedy in the struggle for freedom and the freedom in a tragic predicament. This comic release is the black groan made gay. Yet this release is . . . engaged gaiety, subversive joy and revolutionary patience, which works for and looks to the kingdom to come. It is utopian in that it breeds a defiant dissatisfaction with the present and encourages action. It is tragic in that it tempers exorbitant expectations. This perspective precludes political disillusionment and its product, misanthropic nihilism. . . . Life is viewed as both a carnival to enjoy and a battlefield on which to fight. Afro-American Christianity promotes a gospel that empowers black people to survive and struggle in a God-forsaken land." (Cornel West, professor, author, public intellectual, philosopher)

Invocation

Great God Almighty, we come in gladness, joy, and delight to stand in your presence, making a joyful noise as we exclaim your glory, your power, your generosity. Gather us in a robust manner, so that everything that has breath can shout, "Let us worship God!"

Reflections

Joy, a dynamic energy that accompanies faith, propels us through our day. Joy helps us experience health and spirituality as a whole person. Joy helps shape our attitudes and our mental, spiritual, emotional, economic, and physical well-being. Joy helps us believe we can grow, change, and make a difference. Joy lightens our step and reminds us of probability and possibility. Joy helps us experience the cup as half full, symbolizing possibility and a sense of movement toward reaching a goal, as opposed to a cup half empty, signaling a sense of loss and defeat. Joy interweaves with our life experiences, creating uplifting quantum strands of memories and stories about our walk with God. Our lives in communities help sustain our relationship with God. Joy is infectious and helps us give others a dose of cheer. Joy helps us face the impossible and places us in the mind-set and space of transformation. Joy, shaped by a faithful spirituality, provides the categories where we can sort out our decision making, make choices, dream dreams, and have visions about where God wants to take us with a sense of graced optimism.

Prayer

Merciful Redeemer, we delight that you are the power, the grounds for a healthy, balanced life that combines our prayers, our deeds, and our thoughts together, shaped by grace to produce joy. We give thanks that the net result of a balanced, inclusive, free life in Christ Jesus is the gift of joy. How blessed that joy is a part of many human experiences, including sexual love, marriage, and childbirth, as well as encountering God in history and the nature of worship. We celebrate you, blessed One, that we can know joy in deliverance. We give thanks for the joy that comes with well-being, success, and having the desires of our hearts. Joy allows us to take delight in God, life, and ourselves. In humility, we take delight that to know joy is to know a deep happiness and tranquillity. We are grateful that our joy goes much deeper than happiness. We thank you for our experiences of rejoicing, contentment, gladness, satisfaction, serenity, faith, and hope. With joy incarnate, we have come to a heightened awareness and knowledge of God and self. For this joy, we give thanks.

Litany

Leader: We know joy in many ways, through prayerful living, in hearing the word and in being of value to God as we value ourselves and others.

People: **We know hopeful peace and much ecstasy when we rehear the story of Jesus making a post-resurrection appearance and having a meal with the disciples.**

Leader: Joy occurs with the spreading of the gospel and with our experience of God's rule or kingdom and God's faithfulness in our lives and the lives of those of our community.

People: **Joy, like love, peace, kindness, patience, generosity, faithfulness, self-control, and gentleness are fruits, gifts of the Spirit. Thus we can pray in joy, which brings unity and humility in community.**

Leader: We know joy in the restoration of good relationships. So great is this gift of joy that we can never thank God enough for this gift.

People: **We continue to walk by faith, for even though we have not seen Christ Jesus in his physical realm, we believe in him. Through him, we know indescribable joy, and we get to reflect Jesus to others wherever we go.**

Benediction

As God is the joy of our salvation, let us go forth in praise and laughter to share our experience of freedom and renewal, of balance and love, of hope and faith. God be with you always; go now in peace. Amen.

44. Justice

*But let justice roll down like waters, /
and righteousness like an everflowing stream.*
—Amos 5:24

Quotation

I f my cup won't hold but a pint and yours holds a quart, would-
n't it be mean not to let me have my little half-measure full?"
(Sojourner Truth [1797–1883], preacher, abolitionist,
women's rights worker)

Invocation

Diviner of justice and Deliver of hope, we come to worship, to
praise, to honor the cause of truth, fairness, mercy, and justice!
Let us worship in community, celebrating right relationships.

Reflections

Most of us were reared on principles of fairness and equality: if
you work hard in school, make good grades, and stay out of
trouble, when you graduate you will be able to find a job. We
establish patterns in life that we think work each and every
waking moment. We think that this work mold ought to fit
everyone, and if this work mold doesn't fit someone, then that
person is at fault, because this work ethic is faultless. In our
present economy and social environment, everyone with a
"good" education does not necessarily have a "good" job.
What is a good education and what is a good job, anyway?
Quickly we see that so much of what we assume to be equal
must therefore be fair, and if it is equal and/or fair, we assume
it must be just. And if it is just, it is automatically fair and/or
equal. We think that justice, fairness, and equality mean the
same thing and can be used interchangeably. Justice is an ideal

of moral propriety, or the privilege or power to which one is entitled. Justice can also refer to meriting moral approval or the right to properly claim something as due. Some define justice as the administration of impartial rulings on conflicting claims or the assignment of merited rewards or punishments. Justice may be an opportunity to determine a particular set of rights according to the rules of equity or law. For others, justice implies a fair or due process wherein the outcome is incidental. One key theologically ideal framing of justice is righteousness. By faith, one aspires to live the just life, where making that divine-human connection is a total way of living and embracing salvation.

Prayer

Blessed Savior, in our days of discontent, as we know the loss of innocence and the logic of fairness, let your justice fall afresh so that we may seek redemption and not be lured into danger. Let us not live in denial, crying out, "I didn't mean to cause harm," as though that justifies the harm that we inflict on others. When overwhelmed by difficult decision making, amid creative chaos that can yield countless varied and difficult choices and decisions, help us be mindful of your justice, always yoked with your mercy and goodness. As human beings, we struggle between obedience and disobedience. Please quiet our arrogance. Bolster our poor self-imagery, low self-esteem, and greed. Help us practice justice for justice's sake and not be trapped by deep wounds inflicted on us by ourselves and by others, so that our hearts become heavy with a need and a thirst for revenge or vengeance. You remake us daily to live a just life. Help us stand strong against the temptation to lie, steal, and cheat—the temptation to damage things or people's reputations and good names. Help us work for justice, equality, and fairness. Help us dream, create, and invent for the cause of joy and justice.

Litany

Leader: A life shaped by justice radiates God's righteousness throughout everything we do, creating a beacon of hope, regenerating our health, and feeding our spirits.

People: **As encouraged beings, we rejoice for the wisdom that helps us discern the call God has on us as individuals and as communities of faith, which connects us as ten thousand grains of sand.**

Leader: The inspiring news of a faithful life calls us to justice, revitalizes us, presses us to be all God created us to be, and moves us to confess acts of oppression, to work to transform them, and to encourage others to stay the course.

People: **As motivated beings, we grasp the justice of God that courses through our veins, we sense the brilliance of God that called us into being, and we taste the goodness of God that enlightens our own awareness.**

Leader: The resurrecting news of a faithful life reclaims us and challenges us to be a covenant people seeking justice, loved by God, and chosen by God to stand against injustice.

People: **As spirited beings, we look with new eyes, hear with new ears, touch with new hands, smell and taste in new ways. As part of new justice-based communities, formed for the glory of God and for the edification of our sacredness, we are free from the need to oppress.**

Benediction

As the prophet Amos proclaims the overflowing call to justice, let us go forth to think, walk, and talk the life of justice so that our communities can thrive and live in harmony. God be with you always; go now in peace. Amen.

45. Love

Set me as a seal upon your heart, /as a seal upon your arm; /for love is strong as death, /jealousy is cruel as the grave. /Its flashes are flashes of fire, /a most vehement flame.
—Song of Solomon 8:6

Quotation

L ove, I find is like singing. Everybody can do enough to satisfy themselves, though it may not impress the neighbors as being very much." (Zora Neale Hurston [1901–1960], writer, novelist, folklorist, cultural anthropologist)

Invocation

Beloved God, we adore you as we enter into your gates to give praise and rejoice for your goodness, your blessings, your mercy. In love, fix our hearts and attune us in one accord as we lift our hearts in prayer and praise. Let us worship God!

Reflections

Love—that is, God—is a power and a space that allows us to hold on in uncertainty. Love, a gift of the spirit, lets us stay where we are not wanted until God tells us to move. At such times, love helps us to release all toxins targeted to kill us. Love is an antibiotic to stop the bacteria of sin, provide a cloak of security, and champion an experience of freedom and community. Love is the ark of deliverance, the ship of Zion, the underground railroad, and the source for all journeys from bondage. We often speak of love as *eros*, the erotic; *filia*, brotherly and sisterly love; and *agape*, unconditional love. *Agape* embraces commitment, lets us celebrate peace amid chaos, and ultimately moves us toward reconciliation. Love remains hopeful and joyous, regardless of the lived reality. Love moves everyone and everything to generosity and resolution. Faith embraces all things and nothing. Given our life's choices, and God's choice to love us unconditionally, we experience the generation of new life, we tell the truth, and we move toward healing and wholeness. For those of us who desire, love lets us see in new ways.

Prayer

We give thanks this day for the gifts of a loving God. We rejoice that when we forgot God at times, God, in covenantal love, did not forget us: we are grateful. In the days of our youth and in the days of old age, gird us up in faith and hope, that our lives may exhibit covenantal power and spirit-filled love. Let us never be torn from you, gracious One; let us not descend to the bowels of hell because our love has died. We love you and honor your witness to us and concern for us. We pray that our love is alive in every task of ministry to which we set our hands. May the incarnate love of Christ bless the vision for ourselves, our families, and our churches. May we be loving and faithful as we hold our community members in the highest regard. Let not our hearts be troubled because we feel insecure. Let us come to you with these concerns that you might quiet our fears and strengthen our resolve to love unconditionally. We pray for the graced experience of embracing a love that will not shrink, decline, or diminish. We pray for our congregation, so that we can sustain, embrace, and guide each other by grace, for this day and the next.

Litany

Leader: In the desolateness of foggy days, when grayness surrounds us in the quieted, hidden sun, amid terror and devastation, O God, your love is here.

People: **Gracious God, in love, you have never left us. You have never forsaken us, even when we do not hear you and our pain drowns you out.**

Leader: Your voice echoes in our midst, in loving compassion, like a cool cloth on a feverish forehead, in rippling waterfalls and cool breezes, in great anthems and short choral responses; your love speaks volumes.

People: **In love, God speaks and reveals. In the citadels of vast cathedrals, in the desolation of poverty, in the bastions of education, God is.**

Leader: In the sanctuaries, sacred and secular, great and small: God is. God's love is beyond circumstances, is present in times of horror and joy, war and peace.

People: **May we embrace God's covenant love and total dedication to us, that we might experience love, the love of friend, of romance, of Christ as we experience life as gift.**

Benediction

Beloved saints and children of God, go to serve and share the good news, living in love and charity with your neighbor; go forth to be the embodied Christ to all! God be with you always; go now in peace. Amen.

46. Mercy

And the LORD said, "I will cause all my goodness to pass in front of you, and I will proclaim my name, the LORD, in your presence. I will have mercy on whom I will have mercy, and I will have compassion on whom I will have compassion."
—Exodus 33:19 (NIV)

Quotation

Jesus uses the Samaritan to illustrate that one who was himself an outcast and one of the wounded of society [who] was more likely than the privileged to show kindness and hospitality, which is what compassion means. He is . . . 'the one who showed mercy.' . . . This use of the word mercy I have always thought to be curious in this context, for the word mercy suggests an unmerited kindness, the gift of something undeserved. When a judge shows mercy in a criminal case he is not responding to the facts, or to what custom or even justice requires. Full in the face of justice he shows mercy, that is, he forbears to do what is expected to someone who he has in his power, and who has absolutely no claim upon him of any sort, and instead he shows compassion. It is not simply kindness; it is kindness in the face of the opportunity to do otherwise. Mercy is not less than justice done; it is more than justice requires." (Peter Gomes, Plummer Professor of Christian Morals and Pusey Minister in the Memorial Church, Harvard University, author)

Invocation

Merciful Creator, we enter this sanctuary to offer praises and thanksgiving for your generosity, your grace, and your compassion. For today, and all the days of our lives, you have cradled and nurtured us in covenantal love. In this moment, bring our hearts together in joy and hope, that we might dwell in this sacred place in your glory.

Reflections

We serve a God who is so extraordinary, that we forget to see this extraordinary God in the ordinary moments of life. We forget to be grateful and know joy, because this merciful God pardons our shortcomings daily and does not punish us for the wrongs and transgressions that we commit. While God (unlike many of us) has an eternal memory, God does not hold anger against us for all times; God delights in steadfast love. God fashioned us out of love to be in relationship. When we embrace this relationship covenant in what we do, we know the peace that passes all understanding. God knows us and gives us opportunities to be in prayer and to connect in ways that can afford us a peaceful, gentle way of being. When in intimate relationship with God, we, too, can not only know the depths of God's mercy, but we can also grow in monumental ways, allowing us to express mercy and compassion to others. Mercy is God's gift to us—God's compassion or patience shown to us, even as we stand within God's power, even as we make mistakes and do harm. Mercy is a tremendous blessing, an act of divine kindness or favor. Mercy offers compassionate treatment for those in trouble and distress. As we continue to dwell in God's presence, we will know mercy.

Prayer

Generous Creator, we bask in your love and your mercy as we begin to see the magnificence of you, your creation, and your gifts of love and compassion in this moment. We serve you as a God of abundant love and faith, who blesses us as we bless you and others in return. Your mercy reminds us of our daily call to solidarity and community as disciples of Christ. As we look across time, and across the short days of our habitation on earth, we are moved by your incredible ability to love, and keep loving even when we cease loving ourselves. Your mercy frames the shape of our lives, even as we put ourselves in harm's way. Your mercy is so elegant and sure, so awesome and so simple. For your mercy, which you offer out of love, we give thanks. As we affirm our faith and offer our thanksgiving, we implore you to continue to be the refuge for our souls, for souls everywhere—those who are in danger, those without shelter, those without hope or any persons to care—so that we might all take refuge, and seek your protection and compassion until the destructive storms of our lives pass by. Like your shepherd David, we sing and dance before you, in your mercy, in the great faithfulness of your love, compassion, and concern for all creation.

Litany

Leader: As marvelous as the world God has made, is God's gift of mercy to us that we may know compassion, hope, truth, peace, and a call on our lives to be loving, merciful disciples.

People: **The magnificence of your mercy ever sustains us when we know doubt and fear, when we feel hopeless and forgotten, when the storms of life rage so powerfully that we have no other anchor but you.**

Leader: As a shepherd tends sheep, as a gardener cares for blooming flowers, as a mother hen strokes and embraces her young, so you, O God, have loved and nurtured and tended to our needs from your vantage point of mercy.

People: **Just as the prophets of old told of your judgment and your mercy, we honor those revelations in all corners of our lives; we celebrate and revel in your mercy. We stand in awe and humbleness, with a contrite heart, aware of you.**

Leader: With mercy comes a goodness that is divine, certain, and sure. With blessed assurance, we praise in joy, we praise in gratitude, we praise in anticipation of experiencing your mercy this day.

People: In the rising and setting of the sun, at noontime and eventide, we lift our eyes toward you, as we recall your many acts of mercy toward us, others, and your world, for the salvation of our lives.

Benediction

Beloveds, may all that is just and merciful ever be your companions. May you celebrate God and God's mercy in the many communities where you grow, and love, and live. May this mercy bring you comfort and inspiration in the days ahead. God be with you always; go now in peace. Amen.

—ɷ—

47. Ministry

We put no obstacle in any one's way, so that no
fault may be found with our ministry.
—2 Corinthians 6:3

Quotation

If every black preacher in America decided to confront seriously the status quo through sermons and programs that advocated protest against our cavalier treatment of the poor, we could begin the process of transforming the condition of life for the oppressed of society. This radical approach to ministry would enable the church to reclaim its heritage as an institution that has been on the cutting edge of social change. This radical approach [to ministry] may mean that preachers will have to sacrifice popularity, acceptability, and personal success of the good of the black community as a whole." (James H. Harris, minister, pastor, author)

Invocation

Now is the time for proclamation, song, and dynamic interaction as we enter the hour for praise, adoration, and healing: a living ministry among the people of God. Let us worship God!

Reflections

The faithful life of ministry is a refreshing pilgrimage: one journeys to many places, but returns always to her or his center for perspective and insight. Not only is God the center, but God also stands as a lightning rod, to counter the damage that can be done to various human internal and communal systems. Just as construction workers toil all day in often inclement weather, to lead a faith-filled life is to know the meaning of hard work. Children of faith must be open to God's grace to bring multiple faith ministries to that place of peace and serenity. Peace and serenity are active vehicles for expressing divine compassion. In this kind of environment, everyone learns to respect everyone else and we learn not to take people or God's grace for granted. This grace affords healing, learning, and loving. Ministry involves officiating or assisting in the work of God, by preaching, teaching, and modeling a balanced life of faith; by being involved in church worship, in religious orders, or in chaplaincy; or by participating as an agent or diplomatic representative of God. Not all ministries involve ordination, but they all require commitment, a call by God. Ministry is an opportunity to embrace life, to represent to others the light of God, and to offer a vision of hope, thanksgiving, and possibility.

Prayer

Ministering God, we bless you for the gifts of ministry that offer compassion, care, and concern for your children who know joy and sorrow, hope and despair, freedom yet imprisonment. As you have called us out to model love and possibility, bless us to stay the course as you mold us. Help us be there for others and be fully in attendance in the moment of ministry as a Christ-presence. Help us never feel superior or inferior to any individual because of their particular location and position in life. Let us see the difference between true value and jaded greed. In offering ministry, give us the spirit of generosity that we might treat each person as if we were caring for the Christ. May we also be open to being ministered to by those we minister to, for it is in giving that we receive, it is in sharing that we are filled, it is in seeing that we gain sight. We ask mercy and peace for all who do ministry in local congregations, in hospitals and prisons, in nonprofit and charity organizations, in denominational offices and religious publishing houses that provide us with literature, in ecumenical and interfaith agencies and groups that seek to create bridges between all of God's people of faith. May the joy that we receive by giving cloak us with peace and contentment, new faith, and hope restored.

Litany

Leader: O people of God, let us stand together and rededicate our lives to the ministry of being a Christian, praying for the sick, feeding the hungry, clothing the naked, and preaching good news to all who will hear.

People: **As God is our helper, we rededicate our lives and resources to a ministry of hope, as we are called to be Jesus and let our lights shine wherever we are.**

Leader: O people of God, let us kneel in humility, for God has been so good to us. In the wake of this covenantal goodness, let us minister graciously to all we see.

People: **As God is our helper, we humbly accept the challenge of treating each person with dignity and respect, of being a welcoming presence without judgment or snobbish attitude.**

Leader: O people of God, let us clap our hands in praise when we celebrate the call God has on our lives to model who Jesus is; let us clap our hands in our words and our actions, in our attitudes, and in the giving of our resources of thought, finances, and time.

People: **As God is our helper, we rejoice that we have an opportunity to serve as ministers of God, ordained and lay, as we fix our eyes on our Creator and not creaturely troubles.**

Benediction

And now that we have come and worshiped, been inspired, and shared, we go forth to do ministry, called by God, committed to loving, knowing balance, and honoring peace! God be with you always; go now in peace. Amen.

—〰—

48. Mystery

That their hearts may be encouraged as they are knit together in love, to have all the riches of assured understanding and the knowledge of God's mystery, of Christ.
—Colossians 2:2

Quotation

God is the one who authors the 'eye-opening' and the 'blinding' . . . by allowing the existence of two Spirits, that of Truth and that of Falsehood . . . in apocalyptically [threatening] charged settings; 'mystery' refers to God's interventionist actions in the realm of humankind. Amazingly, while these actions . . . lead some to salvation, they incite in others the kind of hardening that guarantees destruction." (Brian Blount, author, scholar, professor)

Invocation

And now the hour has come for us to stand before God's presence and mystery, in awe and anticipation of the many blessings and the sense of reconciliation that is about to unfold. Let us worship God!

Reflections

Often when we hear the word *mystery*, we think about detective novels and suspense thrillers, or the whodunits of Sherlock Holmes's fame. Rarely is our initial thought about the reality and characteristics of God. A mystery, however, is a religious truth that we can really know only by revelation. We may have a sense about what is going on, but we can never fully understand. Religious mysteries for Christians include the nativity and the crucifixion of Christ. We know how babies are born. We would be scandalized if one of our daughters told us that she was pregnant and the Holy Spirit did it. We would think she was lying. The gospel teaches us that Mary did conceive by the Holy Spirit, and we accept this proclamation on faith. However, we can never fully understand this at all. Mysteries involve profound, inexplicable occurrences. The beauty of God's mysteries is that we do not need to prove the revelation, but embrace it. There is something refreshing about people believing something for over two thousand years that cannot be proved with hard science or forensic evidence, but we profess it to be true. Mysteries unfold each day in our lives, and God wants to do wondrous things for us, if we will only be still long enough in God's presence and wait as our change comes.

Prayer

O noble One, we love you and stand in awe of your great wonders and mysteries. We bless you for delighting in us and for sending Jesus the Christ to live out the gift of incarnate, redemptive love on earth. Blessed are you who give the spiritual gifts that bring us renewed joy and peace. Only you can make clear to us those mysteries, those truths beyond our understanding. We bless the gifts of healing and the working of miracles every day of our lives—the miracles of birth and death, the miracles that occur through prayer and the laying on of hands, the miracles that emerge through the anointing of the Holy Spirit. For the gifts of speaking in tongues or special prayer language, we know gratitude. For the miracle of love and prophecy, the tools of up-building and consolation, of revelation and encouragement, our appreciation knows no end. For the joys and the strength and the healing of these gifts, we bless you, and we yield ourselves to your molding and your blessing. Be with us when we encounter mystery, that we will not fear or worry, but will wait with courage for your revelation and good news.

Litany

Leader: As awesome as the break of day, as romantic as the setting sun, as lovely as a bed of roses, as quiet as the still of night, so is the mystery of God and the possibility of God's people.

People: **In the newness and mystery of today, we bless creation by paying attention, by seeing the colors, hearing the birds, and listening to each other that we might hear the voice of God.**

Leader: As awesome as the break of day, as restful as the incoming tides, as rugged as the sides of mountains, as fleeting as falling leaves, so is the presence and mystery of God, and the mysteries of life.

People: **In the newness of today, we want to see clearly through the fog and the mist of daily schedules that create havoc in our lives; we want to move toward a pace that is better suited for wholeness and joy.**

Leader: As we come into this sanctuary, this consecrated place of God, we stand in covenant with each other, testifying to the glorious hiddenness of God, and our own healing.

People: **As we come into this sanctuary, this mysterious Holy of holies, singing Sanctus, Gloria, we come for renewal, for reclaiming our place as God's children, for reconciling grace that we might be whole.**

Benediction

In honor of the unexplainable mystery and graciousness of God, in anticipation of the revelation of mystery in our lives to come, we leave this worship experience in faith and hope, to experience the light of God wherever we go. God be with you always; go now in peace. Amen.

—m—

49. Prayer

Have no anxiety about anything, but in everything by prayer and supplication with thanksgiving let your requests be made known to God.
—Philippians 4:6

Quotation

Prayer is an attempt to count the stars of our souls. Under its sacred canopy, an oratory of hope echoes the vast but immediate distances between who we are and who we want to be. This peculiar trek sentences its devotees to an arduous discipline. Prayer demands focus and obedience, as well as intimacy and faithful nurture. A certain civility is inherent in this transaction. Its requirements are both communal and individual. . . . Prayer is conversation with God." (James M. Washington [1948–1997], professor, preacher, author, lecturer)

Invocation

Come into the temple of God to offer adoration and lift up prayer, the link between the divine and the human, in gratitude, in request, and for healing. Let us worship God!

Reflections

Prayer is a rather amazing force. Physically, we cannot actually see, taste, hear, touch, smell, or repair it; prayer is not an occasion that is meant merely for our own benefit or limited to special occasions. We can pray together or we can pray alone; we can pray aloud or silently. Even a moan can become a prayer. We can see the results of prayer in the lives of others, as we note the shift from eyes that are glazed over, dull, angered, or depressed, to eyes that twinkle, that light up and say "I am alive and well, and I know the love of God." While we cannot taste prayer as we would an hors d'oeuvre, we can taste the difference in people's attitudes when their persona shifts from being bitter, sour, rancid, astringent, to being fresh, sweet, mellow, and more agreeable to one's palate. Though we cannot actually see prayer and though there are no musical instruments named prayer, we hear the essence of prayer in changed lives, in inspired preaching, in moving rituals, and in the voices of those who prayerfully walk by faith in their intimate relationship with God. We touch faith when we come in contact with those who live a life of "sanctified resistance,"[1] where one stands and lives for righteousness and justice. We smell prayer in the covenant of God that is manifested in the aromas of nature. Only the grace of God can repair

---

1. A term coined by the Reverend Keith Russell, Ph.D., President, American Baptist Seminary of the West, in a sermon, based on Revelation 21:1-6, preached at Allen Temple Baptist Church, Oakland, California, July 11, 1999.

our broken faith when we feel our prayers have not been heard or answered, when we feel tested and tried, and when we are overwhelmed and out of sync with ourselves.

Prayer

Generous, consecrated God, teach us how to pray, when we dance on mountaintops, when we kneel in the valleys, or when we walk along the seashores of life. Sometimes our lives often seem void of shepherds to hold us and lead us out of dark places. Often we wrestle in places near the shadows of death and depression, places of great want and need—unending corridors, stairs going nowhere, endless mazes of pain and dysfunctional behavior that signify the loss of innocence and hope. Even in the midst of such fungus and stagnant hope, green with algae and envy, littered with debris and tormented thoughts, we know you are there with us. We know as we breathe, and move, and wail, and dance, you are with us. You are Immanuel. So in the valleys, amid hills and mountains, we can rest in pastures of passion and peace. We know that when we pray, despite the circumstances, we can experience places of respite, of mercy, spaces where the Shepherd never forsakes the sheep. In prayer, plateaus of confusion become highlands of clarity; chasms of chaos become canyons of joy. As children or youth, we can come to you in prayer. As a group or as an individual we can come to you in prayer. How marvelous that, by grace, we know a continuum of life's experiences. Like streams and lakes and rivers, we flow, intermingling, connecting to oceans of you and me and our community. Your tributaries of salvation meet our triumphs and struggle, in prayer, as together we embark on our quest for the Holy Grail: For you, O God.

Litany

Leader: How glad we are to know that prayer is the key that restores us to a faith that can move mountains that seem unmovable.

People: How blessed that prayer helps us stand the pains that seem to be eternal, the grief of depths unimaginable.

Leader: Prayer, like ambrosia, cools our hearts, our lips, our minds when grief and pain seem to haunt us when we face diseases that ravage our bodies.

People: Prayer lifts us up higher and higher and connects us with the Fountain that brings water and life everlasting, with the Light that guides our pathways for all times.

Leader: Prayer opens us up to God's beauty—a symphonic movement whose music inspires generations, a banquet of food that nourishes our bodies and spirits.

People: Prayer connects us with God when things are quiet or tumultuous, for every breath that we take is like a prayer that gives us life.

Benediction

Prayerful saints, as we leave, let us go remembering to pray without ceasing, to pray in anticipation, in thanksgiving, and in renewal. God be with you always; go now in peace. Amen.

50. Self-Worth

But let it be the hidden person of the heart with the imperishable jewel of a gentle and quiet spirit, which in God's sight is very precious.
—1 Peter 3:4

Quotation

I think I'm just as good as anyone. That's the way I was brought up. I'll tell you a secret: I think I'm better! Ha! I remember being aware that colored people were supposed to feel inferior. I knew I was a smart little thing, a personality, an individual —a human being! I couldn't understand how people could look at me and not see that, because it sure was obvious to me." (Bessie Delaney [1891–1995], dentist; second Black woman to practice dentistry in New York City)

Invocation

Lord God of Abraham, Sarah, Isaac, Rebecca, Jacob, Rachel, and Leah, we come as individual selves joined in community inviting your presence among us as you have been there for the ancients before us. Gather our hearts, spirits, and bodies; make us one as we approach the throne of grace.

Reflections

Sometimes we feel uncomfortable because we think and feel that we are different from others around us. Sometimes these experiences shake our realities, moving us out of those zones where we take life and God for granted. Those are the moments that our self-worth may be shaken. These moments are opportunities for us to show up and embrace life in all its drama, circumstances, surprises, and disappointments. When others have been unpleasant to us, we must often realize that they may be sick or just plain rude. Our job is not to let those we despise, those who seem out to get us, or those who pretend we do not exist affect how we feel about ourselves. As a neighbor in community, we are called to accord them dignity, embracing them not out of masochism, but out of God's unconditional love, which allows us to love without being harmed. We can grow in grace and self assurance, and we can learn to love and like ourselves. This certainty of growth, faith, and love fuels our lives, and gives us hidden power that forms bridges over gaping abysses. By faith, we gain a vitality that defines new spaces where we can dwell, that protects us and lines our prayer closets and brings the gift of life everlasting. The more we love ourselves, the more we are able to truly love God and accept Jesus' invitation, "[If you come] to love the Lord your God with all your heart, and [you will thus be able to] love your neighbor as yourself."

Prayer

Blessed Lord, as we grow in love and grace, and know who we are and whose we are, we experience the power of God. We honor God's ordained resiliency and the creativity of our human brokenness, which allows us great flexibility and possibility. God, as you fuel hopeful transformation, our unhealthy fear evolves into F.E.A.R.—*Facing Every Anxiety Righteously*. O blessed One, when we know who we are and what we are about, and when we love ourselves well and have a strong sense of self-identity, then we are no longer caught in the throes of being victim or oppressor. As this change comes, we are truly able to extol the good news—the God news—both that we are lovable and that we are loved. As lovable beings, our self-worth increases. We give eternal thanks that since you give us the knowledge of love, we have no need to live on the streets of shame and guilt, or be threatened by personal doubts and fears. As loved beings, we know that you continue to love us no matter our sins, errors, mistakes, poor decisions, or stupidities. You are truly the loving Parent who nurtures us when we are empty of love, who gives us divine love when all human love is lost and inadequate for our never-ending needs. We thank you for this knowledge of love, for in this knowledge we learn that our murkiest thoughts and feelings are simply thoughts and fears that have no power to destroy us; we remain safe and secure in your loving arms. We are so grateful that, as we become stronger in you, we come to know that love is enough.

Litany

Leader: Out of the unconsciousness of our collective beings, we celebrate the vitality of community, of self-worth, of life, of being.

People: **Aware of God's salvation and our destruction of self and those deemed other, we honor the sacred within.**

Leader: We focus not on ignorance and woundedness, not on fear and vengeance, but on the beauty and the possibility of transformation within us all.

People: **Because God is still God and is still our God, we are whom God created us to be; we can live out our lives valuing our worth, being true to ourselves and true to you, divine One, without apology.**

Leader: Shaped by intimate, healthy relationships with God, we begin to see and know and learn differently. We learn to like and love ourselves, seeing our illumined beauty.

People: **As our love for self grows, we are able to see fully who we are and whose we are: we belong to God, and God endows us with self-worth.**

Benediction

As our time together draws to a close, may the Spirit bless you and keep you, dwelling among you in your coming and going, as you go about witnessing to others of their self-worth, of their worth to God, and of the blessedness of life touched by God. God be with you always; go now in peace. Amen.

—ᗰ—

51. Soul/Spirit

For thou hast delivered my soul from death, /yea, my feet from falling, /that I may walk before God /in the light of life.
—Psalm 56:13

Quotation

I t is the spirit that knows Beauty, that has music in its soul and the color of sunsets in its handkerchiefs; that can dance on a flaming world and make the world dance, too. Such is the soul of the Negro." (W. E. B. DuBois [1868–1963], professor, sociologist, author, political activist)

Invocation

As we invoke the Spirit of God and our ancestral cloud of witnesses, let us come together in unity, honoring the Spirit within as we embark on our worship journey together. Let us worship God!

Reflections

The "Call and Response" technique, common to many musical and religious traditions of persons from the continent of Africa or who live in the African Diaspora, echoes the nature of our spirituality in an exponential way. Out of our gifts and graces to be human and to be talented, God calls us to respond by living life fully, by calling others into community, and by helping them learn how to respond in love. Being engaged in a loving, nurturing community means connecting to a group of spirited humanity. A soul or spirit is a kind of animating principle or actuating cause of an individual life. Every human being has an immortal spirit/soul that is the invisible, immaterial, intelligent part of a person. God inspirits our bodies; God blesses us and we bless God and each other. The reciprocity of this kind of spiritual call and response engenders a noble connectedness. With respect and dignity, we honor the soul/spirit within all people. The soul/spirit assists one in living a moral life. The role of the community is to nurture, protect, teach, and support the soul/spirit, mind, and body of its members. This support is keenly needed when we are invariably bombarded with issues that put us into rough, hard places. God created us to live in relationships, to live as moral beings, anointed and empowered by the Holy Spirit with thanksgiving.

Prayer

Blessed Advocate, in the places clouded and bleak, we have always known that you would never forsake us. We praise you for creating us as beings with spirit, mind, and body. How blessed we are to be made so complex, so sacred and beautiful. With prophetic imagination, we approach you for a fresh anointing of your wisdom and power. Your blessing of discernment is an ever present, critical tool to our daily walk of love and contemplation. We know that you are ever-present because you promised that you would never leave us alone, nor forsake us. Give us grace and the strength to better model a healthy spiritual life. Help us see that every child is a soul, a spirit to be nurtured. Give us the strength to live a faithful life, modeling to all a righteous, just, and peaceful life. Let us see your light within the spirits and souls of every person we meet. When we are tired and weary, help us know that not only are our bodies stressed, but we are also placing undue stress on our spirits. Please bless us to live in the moment, ever grounding our total beings, particularly our spirits, deep within you.

171

Litany

Leader: Lo, the angels of God proclaim the majestic sweetness that shapes the covenantal relationships, forged for life, between God and humanity for the sake of healthy spiritual, physical, emotional, and mental ways of being and open, loving communities.

People: **In the spirit of civility and justice, we commit ourselves to God and to the rule of God on earth, where transformation is sure and wickedness in our communities is overcome for the glory of God and the good of humanity.**

Leader: Lo, the angels of God proclaim the great faithfulness of God, a faithfulness that endures within our community. We rejoice in God's eternal life and the gift of our spiritual selves, especially as we know sorrow, regret, temptation, and disease.

People: **In the spirit of all that is loving, peaceful, and freeing, we stand in God's presence. In an attitude of praise, we cry out to our holy God: please remember our community at home, at work, and in your sanctuary.**

Leader: Behold the joy and the restorative powers of the Lord, our God, who builds our community, who has the loving flexibility to forgive, who weeps with us in our distress, who girds our spirits.

People: **In the spirit of our ancestors' faith and conviction, we pray to let go of things unimportant, and cherish those things and experiences of value; we pray that we may become a community of witnesses to the world, proclaiming what God has done for us.**

Benediction

Now that our time together has ended, let us recommit to living a just, peaceful, and spiritual life, one that honors your sacred life within us as we go forth into the world to serve our God. God be with you always; go now in peace. Amen.

—⟋∭⟍—

52. Testimony

Then I fell down at [the angel's] feet to worship him, but he said to me, "You must not do that! I am a fellow servant with you and your [brothers and sisters] who hold the testimony of Jesus. Worship God." For the testimony of Jesus is the spirit of prophecy.
—Revelation 19:10

Quotation

Testimony] is a deeply shared practice—one that is possible only in a community that recognizes that falsehood is strong, but that yearns nonetheless to know what is true and good. . . . The testimony given by African Americans is derived from their experience of marginality in the American context. . . . Even though the civil rights movement brought relative justice and ended the universal system of apartheid, the black masses are still caught in a web of selective apartheid . . . the testimony of African Americans has been, and still is, verbalized in preaching, praying, singing, shouting, and storytelling. . . . [T]his has been therapeutic and salvific for the Black church." (Thomas Hoyt Jr., New Testament scholar, Christian Methodist Episcopal Church bishop)

173

Invocation

Come, let us tell the story of love; let us share the story of thanksgiving and hope; let us bring our stories to the altar for healing and reclamation of our heritage and faith! Let us worship God!

Reflections

When we think of testimony, our minds go quickly to court-rooms, those on a television drama series, or those benches where we have sat, either as a witness, an attorney, a juror, or a troubled family member. To give testimony is to tell the truth about an event, to give witness, to offer proof, to give evidence, or to offer a demonstration about some reality. In the Bible, God offers testimony about the character of God and humanity. Scripture gives witness to a desired covenant relationship with God. As communities, we often cry out to God; we witness to God to remember us, and we rejoice, knowing that God has redeemed us through prayers for deliverance. The opportunity to give testimony about what God has done in our lives is to experience God's glory in the restoration of our lives. We testify, for we want others to know our joy and be able to release their fear, for God knows us all by name and wants us all to experience redemption and peace. The opportunity to offer testimony is the gift of sharing the blessing of God's covenantal love. Part of the church's ministry is to go and tell the story of the gospel of the indescribable, incredible joy that comes when one knows God in an intimate, special manner. When we tell our stories, we reveal hope and the place of peace.

Prayer

Giver of life and hope, we give thanks for the testimony invoked by you and made apparent in the Bible. We honor scripture as revelation, and it is by revelation that you inform us and teach and guide us. We are blessed by sharing our testimony, and we affirm that the transformation in us is because of your mercy and grace. Our testimony and those of the prophets and other witnesses in scripture remind us of God's trustworthiness. As children of God called to give our testimony, we live a life of justice, love, and integrity. We testify of the Spirit's witness in us and in all of life. As we share our stories, we pray for the wisdom to know which part of our story to tell, discernment to know when to share our faith story, and courage to tell our story even if we feel uncomfortable. We pray for those who can benefit by hearing the stories of God we have to share. We invite your presence as we share intergenerational stories about new beginnings as we embark into the world, and about our adult and senior moments as we help guide and lead others, ever being refreshed by their eagerness to live their lives in Christ Jesus.

Litany

Leader: Life is a gift! As we tell the stories of our lives, giving testimony to what God has done for us, we help others become open to celebrating their own lives from a gift perspective.

People: **Sharing testimonies acknowledges God's presence and gives life new meaning. That God gives us life and empowers us and shows us favor is a living, covenantal testimony.**

Leader: Testimonies are opportunities to honor all of our healthy relationships. Testimonies invite us to have other relationships transformed, and they give witness to the importance of participating in acts of charity, generosity, and kindness.

People: **All the earth and the fullness thereof is God's testimony of generosity, for God created all of the natural resources necessary to sustain us, and God gave us the brainpower to use these resources creatively.**

175

Leader: The gospel sounds a clarion call for us to stem our tide
           of greed and global heavy handedness, instead offer-
           ing a testimony of stewardship by being better stew-
           ards of our natural, technological, and economic
           resources.

People: **God's testimony to us includes the gift of life each
           day; our lived testimony is to be responsible, do jus-
           tice, love mercy, and walk humbly with God.**

Benediction

We have shared many stories of faith, hope, and thanksgiving.
Let us go forth to love and serve God as we share testimony, the
good news of the gospel, wherever we go! God be with you
always; go now in peace. Amen.

Scripture Index

Subject Index